The Muses Among Us

THE MUSES AMONG US

Eloquent Listening and Other Pleasures
of the Writer's Craft

Kim Stafford

The University of Georgia Press

Athens and London

Published by the University of Georgia Press
Athens, Georgia 30602

© 2003 by Kim Stafford
Designed by April Leidig-Higgins
Set in Monotype Garamond by
  Copperline Book Services, Inc.
Printed and bound by Thomson-Shore, Inc.

The paper in this book meets the guidelines for
permanence and durability of the Committee on
Production Guidelines for Book Longevity of the
Council on Library Resources.

Printed in the United States of America

09 08 07 06 05 P 7 6 5 4 3

Library of Congress Cataloging-in-Publication Data
Stafford, Kim Robert.
  The muses among us : eloquent listening and other
pleasures of the writer's craft / Kim Stafford.
     p.   cm.
ISBN 0-8203-2324-1 (alk. paper)
ISBN 0-8203-2496-5 (pbk. : alk. paper)
1. English language—Rhetoric. 2. Creative writing.
3. Report writing. 4. Authorship. I. Title.
PE1408 .S6667 2003
808'.042—dc21   2002015512

Paperback ISBN-13: 978-0-8203-2496-8

British Library Cataloging-in-Publication Data available

Emily distilling spent days

into an attar of verse. Or Bashō: bamboo.

Or St. Francis, living the life that commands others

to tell his stories. Or a Bard with a mind like mossy

shelves heavy with tales. Or Anansi, spinning creation.

Rumi and Rama spinning spirit. Or Walt Whitman's

mother, to bear such a child. Scheherazade, telling

stories for life, night by night. Or Homer, whose life-

work of two poems is enough. Or on the mountain,

singer of the Song of Songs. Yes, I prefer anonymous—

her naked, indelible call. Your own grandmother softly

putting you to sleep with a hum. Or best of all,

someone we have not yet read, someone wide-eyed,

big-hearted, listening among us now, whose fist

can barely hold a pen.

CONTENTS

PREFACE

From his doting aunt, our son, Guthrie, four years old, has received a child's Polaroid camera. Wrapping paper strewn about him, he turns to my wife, Perrin, and says, "Mom, get with Dad. I want a picture of you to show my children when you're dead." There is a flash, Perrin laughs her tears, Guthrie yanks out the print already beginning to appear, and I reach for the notebook in my pocket to write down what the littlest voice among us has said.

We live many things, we remember some, and we die. That is one version of our story. But for the seeker and the writer, there may be another. This is a book about the imperatives for truth in the life of a seeker, and the sustaining ways of creation in the life of a writer. This is a book about how writers of all kinds may honor the filaments of wisdom spoken by friends and strangers nearby, our local prophets who need our voices to report what they have half-discovered. This is a book about the pleasures of creation as a basis for engaged life in a democratic world—our world threatened by terrible events and uncertain outcomes. In this world, the seeker and the writer find places where something has begun to be said, where greater connections may be anticipated and given voice. What is the role of my voice, this book, and your curiosity in this process?

In a series of first-person letters, essays, manifestoes, and meditations for you, I want to witness what might happen at the boundary called "what you almost know." On the far side, you might have a book, a story, a song or poem or blessing you will write. On this side, you have resonant hunches, griefs, secrets, and confusions. The path from here to there for a seeker requires courage, and for the writer what I call "tricks of beginning," those initially natural but incrementally more complex and sustaining experiments with language that simultaneously honor the voices around you and the voice within you. The act of writing marries the two.

I work at a school in Oregon named for an expedition two centuries old: Lewis and Clark College. My father, the poet William Stafford, taught here before me and left a legacy of writing daily for individual discovery and social reconciliation. He was a pacifist, quiet but also fervent in his practice. My own role at this college for the past fifteen years has been to coordinate the Northwest Writing Institute, a zone for experimentation where we convene to make stories with children, students, adult professionals, and our elders. Many of the writing practices described in this book began as experiments by gatherings of writers there, gatherings disguised as classes called "Writing Your Culture," "Bards of Stumptown," "Voice for Your Tribe," and "Writing for the Healing of the World." In these workshops, the approach has been what this book offers: "What recent learning crowds your mind? What are your richest beginnings? Where do you want to go with those? How can you begin? And as we write, how can we help each other listen deep, begin clear, brave all, and offer our best beyond ourselves?"

When the explorers Lewis and Clark crossed the continent in 1804 and 1805, they were entering a landscape they considered unknown. They went where their maps were blank. But of course the native inhabitants of these lands knew them well. In some ways, this book is a version of the journals those explorers made, but with the greater local reference and democratic reliance that native people knew. I would venture with you into the wide and busy land of creation, into something like Blake's "City of Art," a place where we may celebrate rare specimens of story, lucky sayings of the odd and eloquent, customs of creators we have known, and collections of evocative language gleaned from local inhabitants of all kinds. But unlike Lewis and Clark, my purpose with this work is not a report to my president. Nothing so formal. It is, instead, an offering and an invitation to our time. I believe you and I may share the life of the seeker and the practice of the writer in a world that needs our voices now.

The Muses Among Us

Writing Daily, Writing in Tune

There was a physicist who played the violin. One morning he took his fiddle to the lab, wrapped it green with felt, clamped it gently in a vise, and trained the electron microscope close on the spruce belly, just beside the sound hole, where a steel peg was set humming at a high frequency. Through the microscope, once he got it focused right, he saw the molecular surface of the wood begin to pucker and ripple outward like rings on a pond, the ripples rising gradually into waves, and the steel peg a blur at the heart of play.

When he drew the peg away, the ripples did not stop. In twenty-four hours, the ripples had not stopped. He saw, still, a concentric tremor on the molecular quilt of the wood. The violin, in the firm embrace of the vise, had a song, a thing to say.

In another twelve hours, the ripples flattened and the wood lay inert.

Musicians know this without a microscope. An instrument dies if not played daily. A guitar, a violin, a lute chills the air for the first fifteen minutes of fresh play. It will need to be quickened from scratch. But the fiddle played every day hangs resonant on the wall, quietly boisterous when first it is lifted down, already trembling, anxious to speak, to cry out, to sing at the bow's first stroke. Not to rasp, but to sing. The instrument is in tune before the strings are tuned.

Pablo Casals used to put it so: "If I don't practice for even one day, I can tell the difference when I next cradle the cello in my arms. If I fail to practice for two days, my close friends can also tell the difference. If I don't practice three days, the whole world knows."

Writers know this when they are writing daily. With the first stroke, the hand may swim, the pen glide. The cold glass of the window brightens; the rug has a biography. Sweet tension of silent meeting throbs in the room. Unsaid words grow powerful, wish to speak out. Ideas gather their bones and rise up. A face becomes a life, a place a story. Everything speaks, or is powered by silence. Everything dreams aloud. The pen grows numb with haste, yet calm with plenty.

Yes, there will be labor, and hours with sweat dripping off the elbows. Yes, the words will have to be tuned—but the pen! Already shouting, poised and happy.

SCRIBE TO THE PROPHET

She is dressed in simple gray before us. Into the meetinghouse without image or emblem, I have come with my friends, a group of touring writers. We call ourselves "The Forgotten Language Tour," and we have turned aside from our performance circuit through Iowa to visit the Amana Colony. Our hostess has told us her name is Harriet, and she is here to share with visitors the customs of her people in this cluster of Iowa villages that call themselves "The Community of True Inspiration." I sit toward the back, on the last of the pine benches, which look to have been here at least a century. Everything is plain, quiet. Through the window over Harriet's shoulder, I can see the fields stretching up a gentle slope, and then the sky.

"I remember," Harriet says, "the years of the loud 'Amen!' I remember them well." I feel she must be one of my Midwest relatives, with her welcome of life, of the world, and even of hard change. "We are not better than anyone," she says, "but we were sent here to be in this place." All around us, I feel the open land stretch far away.

"The winds of change are blowing," she says. "Some weeks they are stronger, some not so much, but they are blowing, and we feel them." On the field outside, the wind sweeps along, marking its way in waves across the grass.

"Sundays here at Amana," Harriet says, "the women will enter in that door behind you at the left, and the men in the door behind you at the right. Each comes in order of their age. This has worked well, for the eldest are thus seated in front, where they can hear the service easily." I turn to look at the door for women, the door for men. I am on the women's side.

"You will notice," she says, "if you visit our cemetery, we have no family plots. We are simply laid to rest beside the last brother or sister who has died." I remember the orderly rows of plain markers, the pine needles sifting down from their windbreak trees.

"And when we pray, we kneel on the floor facing the back wall, and lean upon the bench where we have been sitting. We meditate before the sermon. Sometimes I meditate on 'Did I start the beef roast?'—we're not different from anyone else."

She invites us to kneel, and my friends and I smile, turning, kneeling down. When I close my eyes, I see the streets of the little college town where I have been walking at dawn. I see the poster of the army warrior at the post office. I see the statue of the Virgin at the Catholic church. And my brother's sweet face of anguish surges back to mind. Then I hear my friends around me, rising up from prayer.

We turn, and sit again. Harriet picks up a book from the podium in front. "Part of our worship is to read from this book," she says, "our prophecies. We begin with the oldest member reading a passage, and then the book is passed along, until at last the youngest will read. On the women's side, and then on the men's. And this book"—she holds it out to us—"compiles several thousand of our prophecies spoken by what we call the *werkzeuge,* the instruments of divine voice. Our prophets. We have had seventeen of them, one after another. A *werkzeug* might begin speaking holy words at any time of the day or night and must always have a scribe close by to take down these words. If you were scribe, you would sleep in the next room to the prophet's, and if in the night he or she began to speak the voice of the Lord, you would find your lamp and paper, and take down every word."

I close my eyes, and suddenly, I feel a great burden lifted from my shoulders. For it comes to me that I am not the prophet, but scribe to the prophet. When I write, I am secretary to a wisdom the world has made available to me. The voices come from the many around me, and I need more to be alert than wise.

"For meeting, this black coat has been our custom." She puts it on. "And in the old days, black was the dress for brides as well. When my parents were married, the bride wore black. But you know, in 1940 a prospective bride asked one of the elders, 'Might I be married in white, instead of black?' And he was thoughtful for a time, and then he said, 'Yes, that would be all right.' And then she asked him, 'Why has no one at Amana ever been married in white before?' And he thought about that for a time as well. And at last he said to her, 'I guess no one ever asked.'"

I put my hand on the broad pine plank of the bench back before me. What is this gentle combination of long tradition and calm flexibility? The wood under my hand grows warm. Tradition could be like that: an old tree, sturdy, and yet yielding to the winds of change.

"What does the name 'Amana' mean?" someone asks.

"They say it comes from the Song of Solomon," Harriet says, "and is the name of a place: 'Come to the top of high Amana, my beloved.'"

"I remember the years of the loud 'Amen!'" she says again, and something swells in my heart. What is it? What is this familiar tone of her being?

(Later, I learned from my mother that I was often brought to Amana when I was an infant, when my father was studying at the University of Iowa, and we lived in a steel Quonset there. I do not remember those visits, but something stayed with me.)

Today, for me, this resonance is Harriet herself: She is so filled with who she is, and who we are, or could be. Something rises through my body as she speaks of "the loud 'Amen!'" I, too, remember those years of affirmation bigger than patriotism. In my life, they were called the sixties, a time of great freedom that nurtured my generation and also began to kill my brother. Or they were my childhood, when the family was whole, but filled with secrets. Or they were World War II, when my father was a conscientious objector, imprisoned with his comrades in work camps in the California mountains, and my mother the daughter of a pacifist preacher who came to the camps to visit. Or they were the Great Depression, which sent stories forward through time of privation and belief and self-reliant character. Those years when we spoke in a chorus, together—they yet reside within me as I listen to this woman. And they feel possible again, as I listen to the future.

"When a man and a woman begin to think of each other," Harriet says, "the elders see that they are kept apart for about a year. We need to see if their understanding and respect for one another is lasting. They may write to each other, but not meet. Then, if their regard continues to grow, there will be a wedding. And after the wedding, after the cake and wine, and beer, the two young people each go home separately with their parents, while the elders prepare their home of two rooms, their furniture, all they will need. In about two weeks, when all is ready, then they go there together to live."

As Harriet tells of these customs, I find I am looking far away. Far through the window behind her, the grass of the prairie moves as the wind teaches it. The hills take on the colors the sun has taught them. In the college at Grinnell, just down the highway, my brother enrolled in 1966. Something happened to him there he would never tell me. After his death, I learned from my father it had been some kind of initiation, cold in a cornfield, at night. I went to Grinnell to see the world as my brother saw it there. And I met an old professor who told me about Grinnell in the sixties.

"Some of the men's halls," he said, "had what they called the 'Zoo' floor—alcohol, dirt, and pictures—*pictures*. The hazing was *quite* serious. I remember the moment that everything finally changed for the better. As one of the upperclassmen told with clear relish about the cruelty of some of the initiations, from across the room I could hear the president's teeth grinding together, and I knew the hour of change had come."

The following year, the dormitories were reassigned in an alternating pattern—a dorm for women, and the next for men, the next for women, and so on. All that intense male bravado, the professor told me, disappeared.

I held that glimpse of my brother's world. I sat on the pine bench at the back, listening to Harriet tell of old and continuing things. I took into myself, felt my body take in what this would teach me.

I understood that my brother, though a year older, was always too young, too tender, too much the saint. Those were the years of Vietnam, soldiers, a kind of free love for which my brother's Midwest heritage had not prepared him, and his first long departure from home into a world he could not manage.

I understood that the Midwest, cradle of my father and my mother, drew him back, but somehow he did not find the right companions here.

I understood that Harriet was my teacher today, and Amana, among many resonant places, had been my teacher from infancy.

I understood that my mother's father, a preacher, left deep longing in me, a nameless religion of desire and the human word.

I understood that as a writer and citizen, I will be spared the role of prophet. I am like those scribes resting near the prophet, ready to rise up at once and write what speaks. And the prophets are everywhere I turn my listening: the human world, and beyond. The prophets are Harriet, and my absent relatives. My true prophets are dreams, and neighbors, and the sky. I am even scribe to my brother's silence, here in the open country where he once lived.

For these reasons, as I shook Harriet's hand, departing, I was moved to tears. She looked into my eyes.

"You," she said softly, "are a child of Amana."

As I stepped out into the sun, I knew my work.

LIBRARY OF THE MIND

My writing is plagiarized, but not from books. I hear speeches, conversations, and single sentences I want, and often in one pass they remain in my mind, to be transcribed at relative leisure. How does this come to me?

When I first haunted the Cowboy Poetry Gathering in Nevada, I witnessed hours of recitations among the faithful. These were working ranch hands and families from all over the West who found pleasure in sharing poems they had memorized, often without knowing who had written what they knew by heart. After hearing an appealing piece, a listener might say privately to the reciter, "I want that." This did not mean "Where can I buy the book that poem is in?" It meant "I want that in my mind, in my body, where I can get it." Schooled by this urge, I have committed Curley Fletcher's "The Strawberry Roan" to memory:

I was layin' around town, spendin' my time,
I was out of a job, wasn't makin' a dime,
When up steps a feller and says, "I suppose
You're a bronc rider by the looks of your clothes. . . ."

I came away from this tradition with a perverse trick. When in the company of the erudite—say, at a college or library program—I sometimes weave into my presentation a fragment from Shakespeare, and when I lose my way, I appeal to the audience to help me with the next line:

> If music be the food of love, play on;
> Give me excess of it, that, surfeiting,
> The appetite may sicken, and so die.
> That strain again! it had a dying fall:
> O, it came o'er my ear like . . . like . . .

But when I ask for help, no one knows the following words. On one occasion, someone shouted from the back, *"Macbeth!"* No, not *Macbeth*. When they can't help me, when they can't stand it, I give them the rest from the opening lines of *Twelfth Night:*

> . . . like the sweet sound,
> That breathes upon a bank of violets,
> Stealing and giving odour! Enough, no more:
> 'Tis not so sweet now as it was before.

Then I speak my witness about the custom of the cowboys: Among the faithful, if the reciter hangs up on a line, loses the thread of the poem, typically half a dozen listeners will quietly cue the next few words. This is a kind of literacy rare among my academic kindred. So buckaroos, actors, singers, and a few literary obsessives know how to memorize. What happened to the rest of us?

Most of my students have a repertoire of texts from family lore, songs and stories, proverbs, names for place and person, recipes, rules never spoken but universally known within the familiar circle of home. From my own family, I could not help but memorize snatches of informal literature I heard often as a child:

> When we consider Providence, we must admit it's fair,
> That some are given brilliant minds, while some have curly hair.

That from my mother, with whom I share the fate of curly hair. I had, and I believe we all have in some way, early practice in memorizing such things. It's not about an effort of memorization, perhaps, but the benefit of frequent hearing. This along with the standard essential repertoire of playground poetry like "Sticks and stones will break my bones but words will never hurt me." Such a repertoire seems to be a natural part of being what the English language in the ninth century called a *reord berend,* a "bearer of speech," that is, a human being.

As an adult writer, I find my fascination with memorizing the language events around me to be unusual among my colleagues but essential in my own practice. Someone asked, during a panel at a literary conference, "Do you have a computer yet?" (Obviously, this was years ago, when computers were a novelty. Remember those days?) That word "yet" nettled me: "Do you have a computer yet?" The implication was that *every* writer must have a computer, eventually. Among writers on that day's panel, the range of opinion was instructive. One argued strongly for a favorite electric typewriter, while another scoffed at that, repeating the old Mickey Spillane idea that you could only be sure your writing was sincere when your vigor popped every *o* out of the paper by your forceful strike on the platen—only a manual typewriter would do. Then we heard from the advocate of pens, particularly fountain pens, and of the odors of their inks, followed by the devotee of the pencil, preferably a number two with a healthy eraser. "Only a writer who knows how to erase will spare us the bad lines."

After listening to all this, I found myself alone in my vote for oral composition, in the manner of Wordsworth and the poet Caedmon, mythically the first poet in English, who did not know how to write and so chanted his lines extempore. They say the physical act of writing gave Wordsworth dyspepsia, so he preferred to compose in mind while sauntering. I remember reporting to my skeptical friends on the panel that I sometimes find myself chanting a text into being, then repeating and refining it, while out walking or pedaling my bike. There's a nice help from the rhythm of the body to get the text going—a rhythm I find absent at my desk.

They say Mozart could return from the concert hall and jot down an entire symphony from memory. How did he do it? He could remember every note because he understood how they all went together, and to me this is the secret for remembering spoken literature from daily life. Rhyme helps, of course, and repetition. But what about a nonrhyming sentence, the kind of extravaganza that unfurls smooth as water from the tongue? Often, I suspect, these prose treasures, particularly from my elders, are the result of frequent repetition and sifting down to essentials that has found some memorable, internal logic to the words. The utterance has become a fundamental, exemplary sequence in the language, with its own intrinsic structure. Sometimes I have to reconstruct details, but the spoken flourish stays with me verbatim. Occasionally I feel like a single, breathless treasure, stowed in my mind, will be the snubbing post for a whole essay to follow, as when a thin gentleman in a Wyoming café volunteered the following to me:

> Son, you can go down to the variety store and get yourself a little, bitty alligator no bigger'n a lead pencil and feed it bits of hamburger every day for a hundred years and it won't grow at all, but you start giving it whole hamburger patties on a plate and it'll turn into a goddamn monster overnight, and that's just what happened to our federal government!

That, for better or worse, will be with me to the end. It simply has a structure that will not falter from the mind. Each idea is rooted in an image, and each image leads to the next. (William Carlos Williams:

"No ideas but in things.") The speaker's method of composition matches a listener's method of recollection.

I'm probably saying something obvious here—the working logic of memorization—but I think the importance of this activity is not so obvious. I want to learn from my elders in the world and be their scribe. I want to bring particular treasures of the spoken voice into published literature. This seems essential to full inclusion, to honest democracy. An old Eskimo woman paid me a great compliment once, when we were way out on the tundra picking fish from her set net. She had been watching me write many little things in my pocket notebook, ask her for detail, and turn my head to listen with care.

"The *kass'aq* [Cossack, white man, outsider]," she said, "reminds me of many things I have been taking for granted."

Someday, I hope to be an elder. To be ready, I need to take the world into my body and keep it there in neat bundles of words. When I am very old, I need to still remember what my daughter said when she was small:

Did you know God made all the good things? Only men made the bad things, like jails, and bad TV shows. God made the good things, like toy stores. And best of all, he made us grow by giving us protein. Is it hard to die? Because when you die, you know you are being born.

THE WRITER AS PROFESSIONAL EAVESDROPPER

Reading the classified section in Mexico City's *Tiempo Libre,* I came across the notice for an unusual public service:

> Hospital of the word: emergencies and preventative attention. Permanent workshop for the defense of the Spanish language . . . consultations . . . conferences . . . intensive therapy . . . clarify doubts . . . first time assistance.

This anonymous writer was nudging me toward a way of seeing my work, giving me a name for my practice. Maybe my notebook is the hospital of the word, and I practice my roving services by being what in Spanish is called *un fisgón,* a listener, eavesdropper, caretaker of gossip. Maybe I am this gatherer of treasure, shepherding words, phrases, and texts of character orphaned by the world's attention to money and fame.

How was I first recruited to this cause? As a freewheeling writer of poems and personal essays, I hold a dark secret: I was once a scholar—a medievalist. I was that awkward figure haunting libraries, poring over glossaries, thumbing my *Beowulf* and my *Pearl* to rags. I have written twenty pages on the use of the feminine pronoun in a single stanza of an obscure poem from the fourteenth century. Working sleepless through nights to dawn, I have heated cold rooms with the sheer stamina of my reading. I have internalized the nuances of suffixes in ancient texts so that my voice can recite what I no longer understand. That was a long and wonderful training for something I don't do now.

Now that I write, what do I do with that training? Now that I teach writing, how does my scholarship pertain? For both writing and teaching, I now turn that tireless scholarly attention to the flow of language that surrounds me in the world. I read talk. I annotate conversation. I catalog graffiti. I savor the traveler's fictions in bus stations, the tipsy confessions of the midnight lounge car on the train. I long for the banter of hitchhikers recounting their rides and destinations, the semipublic narratives in the booths of coffee shops. I scribble and study conversations at the White Horse Tavern in Greenwich Village, Molly's at the Market in New Orleans, the twenty-four-hour Elkhorn Café in Jackson Hole. I record fictions spoken at the Burns Brothers Truck Plaza south from Portland. I take the corner booth, hunch over my coffee, and listen both ways, tuning in to the periphery of my hearing. I revel in speeches flaunted at the Acropolis Diner, in Brooklyn, as I once absorbed the annual publications of the Early English Text Society.

I live in the modern world, but my habits are older. In the medieval period, books were so rare they were memorized. Travelers took turns reciting favorite texts. The feast of stories exchanged by the pilgrim band in Chaucer's *Canterbury Tales* exaggerates a social custom that was actual. For people living in an oral tradition were poorer in books but richer in stories. Habits of making and sharing stories were different in a way hard to appreciate since Gutenberg. Without books, newspapers, the Internet, junk mail, or radio, everybody lived by spoken stories, from sermons to ballads to jokes to proverbs to the kinds of stories Chaucer's pilgrims exchanged directly with one another.

The first book with pagination didn't appear until the fifteenth century; people *knew* the books they owned, could say them word for word. Chaucer's contemporary John Gower apparently had only eight books in his personal library; he had memorized all eight, however, and he wove quotations and adapted sentences from them throughout the three books he composed himself (one in Latin, one in French, and one in English, because no one knew which language might prevail). But as Socrates had warned his students, once we learn how to read we may forget how to remember. Gutenberg imprisoned literature, and schools maintain the tyranny. How can we join the world again—the ancient permanent human world of literature alive in public life?

As I walked past their ditch on a cold day, I overheard a steamfitter down in the earth say to his partner: "As the world around us grows colder, sincerity and honesty must be the fire to keep us warm." I was on my way to the faculty convocation and paused to jot this worker's sentence in my notebook. But when I reported these words to my colleagues, they refused to believe I had overheard them. "You're a writer," said one. "You made that up." "Where did you really hear that?" said another. "Oh," said a third, "maybe that was one of our English majors who couldn't get a real job."

As my friends honored my skill but insulted my source, I realized poetry in our culture has been exiled from daily life by the claim it is the royal prerogative of the highly educated. Only professors and their students, it would seem, know eloquence. What a shame. Wordsworth, I have been told, has said the most evocative poetry will be spoken by common people in moments of deep feeling. I think he was right.

What shall you and I make of this? As the world grows colder around us, it seems likely I will not hear anything better for some days. Sincerity and honesty—how can we live by these? How can we write and teach by these? What am I to make of my professor friends, their cynicism about language, and about humanity?

Some of my colleagues in the language-rich professions of teaching and writing admit they overhear such occasional gems, but they often explain them away. They believe literature resides in libraries, and students pay tuition to learn secret ways to consume it and perhaps to create it. Writing, in their view, is an esoteric craft to be practiced by the few; I believe such creation is a universal right and talent of my neighbors everywhere. As a writer—and eavesdropper—I know that genius lives where the language lives. Some witness it, overhearing by chance. I eavesdrop professionally, because such listening makes life a perpetual feast, and because I'm not always smart enough to invent things as powerful as what I hear.

Another way to say this: By listening to the glories of conversation around me, I am moved to write, and I am reminded to listen closely to my own most quiet thoughts and dreams. In their inventive talk, my wise neighbors give me permission to take seriously my own internal voice.

In my experience, all pleasure in writing begins with a sense of abundance—rich knowledge and boundless curiosity. A student writer, or a professional journalist, can get by with spare resources, but cannot thrive. Anyone can begin with just enough information to fill a required writing assignment. Writing then will feel like an examination. Or, with abundance, it can feel like flight. And for me, flight begins with the fat little notebook in my pocket. I urge my students to record the hum of talk around them and to bring overheard fragments to class so we may revel together. I urge them to attend to the common muse. Chaucer delights me, but Chaucer is not my muse. Published literature is not my muse. For the muses are all around us. They seem ordinary but are very busy, very generous. I listen everywhere, hush my companion when a good story drifts into range, pull out my notebook and smile.

"Hold that thought," I whisper, "for a moment."

I make my notebooks two and three-quarters by four and a quarter inches, from two full sheets of paper folded small, slit, and sewn into brown cover stock with black thread flavored with beeswax. The little book is a plain and fragrant object. I fold it open to the next fresh page and slip it into my shirt pocket beside my pen. I make up a dozen notebooks at a time, stick my address label on the inside cover of each, and date them as I begin. A stamp decorates the outside cover, usually that old one-cent stamp with the pen and inkwell that proclaims, "The ability to write—a root of democracy." Such a notebook lasts me from a week to a month. Every few months, it's time to sit down with a stack of notebooks and glean the best stories, sayings, and thoughts, and I file these with works in progress according to their particular magnetic attractions. Or when I am given a writing task by an editor, instead of staring at a blank page to gather my thoughts, I leaf through the little notebooks to be reminded of many rich beginnings. The question then is not "What shall I write?" but rather "Which, of the many beauties in my notebook, do I wish to carry forward?" The writer thus sits down to a feast every time, and never to an empty bowl.

My own writing routine surges in a stream of notebooks, letters, and drafts of stories, songs, and essays, all in simultaneous development. A certain amount of chaos flavors the whole rush. In class, I suggest my students catalog their eavesdropping into key categories: conversations overheard, informal speeches, written texts from the street, and graffiti and short phrases. One might label sections of the notebook by these or similar categories, but in my own practice I don't. I take it down as it comes, and organize it later, selecting the best for current work and letting the rest undertake the yeasty work of time on the shelf, in the drawer, in the mind. From such external voices, my students and I move to eavesdropping on our own dreams and our fleeting thoughts. I am an informal folklorist in the world, and a forthright internal eavesdropper. I encourage my students to conduct fieldwork on their own cultures and themselves. Together we take dictation from the world.

Conversations Overheard

Preparing to write an essay, I find, takes a few rich days of eavesdropping, and then some writing time. The writing life has a continuing rhythm of listen and tell, listen and tell. In the world, I find myself barraged by rich conversation. I was sitting in a bar in Philadelphia, late one November evening, when I set down in my notebook this conversation from two regulars in the next booth:

"So, you're going to be a father—when?"

"March."

"You going to be a husband, too?"

"Don't know. Maybe summer."

"Maybe, huh? You don't know, or she don't?"

"I don't."

"Ah!"

What can I do with that? The characterization strikes me as very rich, very concise. Because all questions are not answered, there is room for a story to grow.

There is a similar challenge to the writing life as I savor the sentence I overheard at an education conference: "You know the old saying in surgery: The operation was a success but the patient died." I savor the line I overheard on a plane out of Cheyenne: "Danielle Steele? Oh, she's okay if you're on a cruise and the pool is full." I savor the lament by a cop at the café, as he put on his hat to go out into the rain: "Well, I guess I better get out there and fight crime, and sin, and lust, and pestilence. I keep fighting, but I never win. Oh well—God! It's raining, too!"

What I do with such fragments, again, is to wait, to ponder, to try out provisional uses in letters and postcards to friends. Either several will group themselves naturally to spark an essay, or they may open a poem, invite a story to begin, or simply enrich my abiding pleasure in the language and whet my hearing for more.

Informal Speeches

I sat on a stone bench outside the downtown library in my native city of Portland, Oregon, listening as a street musician named Gypsy Slim, who had camped between two shopping carts for some months, harangued the pedestrians.

"I been to college," he proclaimed to a woman who had paused to consider him, "majored in physics, minored in philosophy, and all the scientists will tell you the temperate zone is the most healthy—regular seasons, hot and cold. But I don't care if it's house, job, creed, ethnic group, country, institution, or sex—they *all* try to stifle what *you* can be! You want to *know* what you can be? Get outside all those categories and have a look!" Then his saxophone wrangled the air, and pigeons scattered, and the woman and several other gathered listeners tossed quarters into his hat and moved on.

On my stone bench, I put down the book I had been reading, and took out my notebook to get Slim's list. Because he had repeated this speech many times, it had developed a rhythm and an order that made it possible to remember: "house, job, creed. . . ." It all fit. If I wrote fast, and soon, I could get every word. It took him, the outsider, to tell us all something true about ourselves. And it took me to take his words down.

Several weeks later, Gypsy Slim disappeared. Now it has been years, and the pedestrians walk freely up the north side of Taylor Street. I brooded over his words, repeated them to friends. Troubled by his passing, I found myself writing a poem called "What Ever Happened to Gypsy Slim?" The poem quotes a part of his harangue. I wrote an essay called "Local Character," in which Slim's speech sets the keynote for a host of eccentrics teaching hard truths to the communities they inhabit. I wrote a short story called "A Dancer on Salmon Street," in which Gypsy Slim's words help a fugitive from office work begin to change his life. Many heard him speak; I took it down, and I study what he said by writing variations on his words again and again.

As a writer, I am aware of ethical issues involved in borrowing texts from strangers. I take these issues seriously. If I can't find Gypsy Slim to ask his permission before quoting him, am I a thief? My students ask me this, and I ask myself. It would be very wrong to use Slim's words irresponsibly. But it would also be wrong to ignore his words. I take the risk of cautious use because I believe in the importance of what he said to all of us. Sometimes my eavesdropping may get me in trouble. But if we don't listen, if we avoid the issue and borrow only from books, we are all diminished.

Gypsy Slim's speech found its way into my writing. Other speeches haven't—yet—but I live by their verve, their ready potential. Take the celebratory recollection by a gentleman I met at a nursing home:

They ain't much difference, yes, between a square and a round dance. They ain't much difference. I been in every state in the New-nited states, and Missouri's the best one for music I was ever in—don't you worry! Why, the caller starts a-callin' and everybody dancin' and if a feller gets lost the caller goes and grabs him and starts him off again! I used to know 'em and call 'em. I ain't called one in probably ten years:

All to your places and straighten up your faces—
Promenade away!
Return to your partners all—

Swing 'em if you love 'em
and cheat 'em if you don't!
Yes sir, right in Missouri—don't you worry!

I accept this gift. It is one of the most breathless enthusiasms I have known. It gives me permission to stretch and listen to the next celebrations that may arise in my own voice.

Written Texts from the Street

There are private ways to publish. You can pay a printer to print your verse and then hawk your own books, which some call vanity publishing. Or you can staple your work, anonymously, to telephone poles, which I call generosity.

In Tijuana late one Halloween night, I found a ballad nailed to a pole. The song was called "Mi Tijuana Querida," a loving ballad to the city itself. I stood in the dim light taking that text down, including the sentence in small writing at the end, which I translate, "You can't pay for this—it is for you."

In Portland, I lifted a letter pasted to the sidewalk by rain beside a pile of someone's earthly possessions flung from an upper-story apartment window. The compact story in that handwritten note pleaded with my heart,

> John—Don't call Uncle Sammy anymore. Their fed up. Owe them money for phone calls. . . . You make mom cry so much she worried sick. Your driving her to an early grave. Work. Work. Work. Pray, pray, pray. Write letters. No calls.
>
> —Violet

What shall I do with these texts the world has sent me? There is a privacy in them, and a sufficiency to the moment of finding them. But

I also feel the impulse to listen to the lives behind them, be their courier. With these two, I don't know yet. And I feel in this "not knowing—yet" the excitement of the writing life. I have a trove that might tell the world spirited things, but I keep this trove in the drawer for now, wishing to use it well. Something in my life will tell me what to do.

In Oregon, there is a group of friends who call themselves "The Homeless Waifs Holiday Club." The group was formed in the 1970s when a generation of college students realized they weren't going home for Thanksgiving, and so banded together for their own invented revelry. One of their customs is to gather at a remote place in the Oregon desert on the first Saturday following the first full moon following the fall equinox for a rousing game of Capture the Flag. No newsletter, no calls, no e-mail—just that fixed annual date.

So there they were, come from all directions (some traveling three thousand miles) to stand in a circle in the dust while the man they called Reverend Whippoorwill, who had thrown the *I Ching* in advance, read the judgment he had composed (he later sent me a copy):

Going out and coming in without error.
Friends come without blame.
To and fro goes the way.
On the seventh day comes return.
It furthers one to have somewhere to go.
After a time of decay comes the turning point.
The powerful light that has been banished returns.
There is movement, but it is not brought about by force.

He read, we stood in silence, then the piano began to play—the piano in the back of the pickup truck starting up the dusty road, with Ronald and Nancy Reagan in festive effigy tied upright against the tailgate, dogs with bandanas around their necks following our ragtag parade, and the thirty-pound cake shaped like Oregon (the west half organic flour, the east half Betty Crocker) carried on a door by four of the faithful.

> The transformation of the old becomes easy.
> The old is discarded and the new is introduced.
> Both measures accord with time.

I suddenly saw the whole spectacle through the wide eyes of a baby bouncing on his mother's hip, as she danced with the parade, shaking her tambourine.

> Walking in the midst of others, one returns alone.

My devotion to such a text is not based purely on its "poetic" quality, though that is there. I pledge allegiance to such a literary offering utterly clean of a search for money or fame. In a world where a photograph of Albert Einstein is used to sell a computer, and where jazz in the public domain sells coffee, homegrown language is restorative, and my calling is clearly to be the recording friend.

Graffiti and Short Phrases

We are surrounded by bits of wisdom and humor, puns, proverbs, jingles, little prayers, short phrases that can go suddenly deep in the midst of the passing flow. A writer takes them seriously by taking them down. It is important for me to know that someone at my college has written on the wall of a restroom stall, "How do you define success in college? Being as intelligent when you get out as when you started." I struggle with the sentence on the bedroom wall of a friend, a teenager, after his suicide: "Due to budget cuts the light at the end of the tunnel has been turned off."

What does it mean about American culture that a shirt at Nantucket proclaims, "He who dies with the most toys wins," while an Idaho bumper sticker holds, "My wife, yes, my dog, maybe, my gun never"? I live with these short texts of American literature, give them a second chance to work on my mind by copying them into my notebook and then returning to them as a basis for writerly meditation. The notebook becomes my devotional book of hours, where the hand-painted sign by a house in a poor neighborhood could launch a short story: "This is our home please dump your garbage elsewhere!" The words etched in the rearview mirror of a car could tease me into an essay about time and change: "Objects in mirror are closer than they appear."

Such passages might be the invisible ink that starts a story, never to appear verbatim in the text, but giving my writing a launch. Or they might actually appear in stories, poems, or essays. But always the prevailing habit of listening and cherishing such gifts will lie behind the solitary work of the imagination, inviting all secrets forward into the light. In daily writing practice, such phrases work like visible catalysts to bring the invisible story into being.

Sometimes I think my muse is a mute elder pleading my attention: My mother's parents lived with the earth in primitive ways (homesteading the high plains of Wyoming ninety years ago); my mother told me stories from that time; and my work is to tell *how* these stories have come to me. I might begin, "My mother showed me her mother's diary from 1911, which begins 'Harrison built our house today, and in the evening sawed out a nice window on the south side.'"

The text comes to me as a gift, and my work is to tell how it arrived, and what it says, and what this saying may imply or call into question. In a similar way, I might say to my students: Find an utterance from the world that seems to address you, and then write an essay telling the story of how that text arrived in your life, and what happened to you as a result of its arrival.

Gifts of rich lore surround us all. While others seem to observe these offerings on occasion and by chance, noticing and then letting them go, I make the hearing and recording of them my mission as a writer, and a key invitation to writing students. Dreams get away if we don't tell them, or write them down. Thoughts do the same. The writer's greatest chance may be devotion to the passing fragment. It is small, but it is pure, and it may hold a compact infinity. You heard it for a reason.

Live Free or Die

The conference was a fine one, where the Wyoming Council on the Arts had gathered us in Casper to wrestle the issues and opportunities of the art trade. But after a couple sessions my head got full and I had to get out. I went softly out the ballroom door, down the motel corridor, across the dusty-white parking lot out back, up the embankment to the railroad tracks, and west. I had to get dust on my shoes and sage in my nose. I had to seek something older than my kind. At the trestle, I scuffed down from the tracks into the willows.

My shoes got muddy and I found a path. I sought the hobo jungle, for surely here, where the train tracks met the North Platte River, travelers would camp. I was afraid, yes. I'm not well schooled in the customs of such places, but I had to learn. My own path joined other paths, all converging at the bank. And there, yes, the hut.

A beaver had felled and bucked a twelve-foot willow log, and some vagabond had set this beam horizontal between two forked trunks, then sewn together a cardboard house with orange baling twine. There was no west wall, leaving the flimsy room open to the fire pit just outside. A grill hung from a branch. A fork lay on a stone. Yet the place was abandoned: Dry leaves had blown into the fire ring. It was late October, but on the feedlot calendar nailed to a tree, the September page still showed a cowboy "Shipping Cattle in the Fall." Already, I liked this citizen the chill fall wind had sent south by highway or by rail.

Inside the hut, a roll of purple carpet formed a pillow for the bed of straw. A strip of canvas just the size of a sleeping form lay ready. I crawled into this room and lay down to sense what such a life might be. I could see the river sliding east toward the Missouri, the last leaves of willow and cottonwood swiveling in the wind. Then I looked up at the cardboard ceiling, where a magazine photograph of Miss Twin Volcanoes stared down at me, where she was pasted, smiling and kind, and I thought suddenly of the Sistine Chapel, of Michelangelo, religion, love, music, all things naked and fair, clear and passionate. I thought of this vagabond who had made from beaver's work and the city's waste his own home in the willows. And then he went away.

The tall blue sky had darkened. I stood just at the edge of the day's light, watched the river gleam and the downtown city lights of Casper looming up on the opposite shore. Then I turned to trudge back toward the conference. I was listed on the program, soon, and would be there in time.

In the gathering dark, before crossing a patch of ground thick with tumbleweeds toward the motel, I wanted a walking stick. Under the trestle, where travelers had built fire and cooked their black-eyed peas in the can, I rummaged through the firewood debris and came up with a stout and knobby shaft. My hand closed over the smooth end.

I turned it over in the dim light. It was hickory, maybe, or holly— some heavy, quirky stuff—with many miles of fist polish on the handle, and with a message whittled in block letters along the shaft: LIVE FREE OR DIE. The letters were carved neatly into the wood and blackened, I guessed, with shoe polish. The owner must have lost this in the tangle of firewood, and gone on south without it. Could I take it? I had lost my knife the week before, my Old Timer. Does it work that way? The trade felt right. I struck the earth with that stick and set out through the tumbleweeds.

It felt right, too, to return at the motel's back door, the trade entrance, to prowl the corridors where steam pipes ran and racks of linens waited, to enter the conference room quietly from the rear and ease into a chair with my hat pulled low. Gradually, I was there, the stick beside me.

As I joined the conversation again, there was talk of getting published, getting artwork into galleries, getting grants, getting recognized. I tightened my grip on the text in my hand. "LIVE FREE," it said. I'm afraid that could mean free of success, if success cut the roots of life. For life can be lost a little at a time, when it goes wrong, and restored a little at a time, by vigilance and creation.

That night I lay in my queen-size bed, heard long-haul trucks sail by outside on I-87, heard wind hammer the motel wall. Streetlight fit through a curtain slot. No river sound. No woman on my ceiling. No Sistine Chapel, music, poetry in this place. I would have to listen deeper, and craft freedom in my own language, from the lives around me. I would have to find the common things in my own place and speak for them. I would have to start with what I was learning now, this moment, and whittle my message.

In the morning, as I set out along the highway west at dawn, my shadow and the shadow of that hobo stick uncoiled along the road half a mile before me.

Quilting Your Solitudes

A Letter to My Class

The other night in class, I heard from each of you why your busy lives have kept you from writing. It broke my heart—especially since I share your predicament and had to confess a dry spell of my own. What shall we do about time and our writing?

Life is a river of stories. Time is a storm of many flavors. What net can catch them? What is the tool, the flask, the spoon for sipping? What is the process to funnel the galaxy of language and story to the writing nib now?

When I watch a great beech tree in a gentle rain, one leaf twitches alone, then another leaf swivels in the great stillness, then another. Looking up from inside the green dome, I begin to learn how my own mind works. One thread of thought wakens, then another, and far away another. There is great reach between glimmerings. How do they find each other? How do they gather and recognize their kinship, these ideas? They find each other during those rare stretches of writing time that come to me, when I can sit still long enough to invite the full spectrum of the possible. And what about most of the time, in the daily rush? My writing would be doomed if the realm of writing were limited to long stretches of solitude. They are too rare. But good luck comes also in sweet morsels of tranquility lasting only a few seconds. My life of writing is rooted in the fragment. And the tiny notebook is my tool.

All coherence in my writing begins in the ready hospitality of the little notebook I carry in my shirt pocket. Because the book and pen are always there, and because my memory is weak, I take dozens of moments each day to jot phrases from the flow of life. I take down a conversation overheard, notes on a sweep of fragrance, an idea that brims up. During a committee meeting, I take dictation on my day-dreaming mind to catch a few quick connections in a story I started last week. While I'm on the phone, I hear myself reporting a remark by a student that will not leave me, and flip open my book with my free hand to write it. At dinner, it comes to me I have been trying all day to record a dream. I put down my glass, take out the book, and get the key phrase stored for later. And sometimes, just before sleep, as the busy buzz of daylight loosens its grip, I heave my body up-right, turn on the lamp, and pour a few insistent words onto the little page.

Coherence is born of random abundance. Memory begins by re-leasing my attention from the official task at hand. The palm-sized book folded open is where every piece of my writing has its begin-ning. Some twinkle in the language around me makes me raise my head, listen close, and jot.

Writing the Little Pieces that Please You

If I examine my own experience, I find the process of writing the lit-tle pieces that please me happens in some variation of the following sequence: finding freedom, using my little notebook, writing a post-card, expanding to a letter, jotting a further gathering of ideas, finding a title, writing the draft, hearing the musical key, expanding, getting response, revising until the piece needs to escape my meddling, and then submitting for publication. I offer these my quirky habits for your own consideration and experimentation. Some works happen in a shorter compass, but this full sequence is available, and may keep us going in manageable increments during the rush of life.

1. FREEDOM

"Creative people," reports my friend Ojeda, the jazz musician, "are people comfortable not knowing—yet." Freedom means not knowing, yet staying alert. Writing begins in the body. The sensitive instrument of the body must be poised before language, the first note, speaks. As my father said, "you can usually be free some of the time / if you wake up before other people." Often, for me, this means a kind of bifocal attention. I listen to the official discussion of any committee I'm on, but I also listen to what is not being said, what is implied but not overt, and even what is said but not heard. Freedom means hearing what it means when a colleague says, "Here's an idea I'd like to toss into the wringer." ("Wringer"? Isn't it "Toss an idea into the ring," a festive circus metaphor? The "wringer" will crush ideas.) I reach for my notebook to take down what I heard.

2. THE NOTEBOOK

In solitude, or in the throng, a few words come to you. They may not seem the right words, but you welcome them. The writer's prerogative is to take small things seriously. A glimpse, a flicker of recollection, an evocative phrase of a few syllables spoken by someone near you. So you take down observations and ideas in the moment they arrive. The small notebook welcomes small ideas, and compact ideas grow in their own way as you write. First you find them worthy, though small; then you let them grow into shapes that others may find worthy. You relax into total hospitality, you gather scraps with no great claim. You begin as a connoisseur of whispers. And this little solitude could be in the midst of a rush before a deadline, on the bus, at the party. All kinds of moments—short, many, always.

If I check my pocket notebook today, I find random lines in which, for some reason, I have faith:

—could you feel raindrops so completely you would polish them?
—how to teach a class: laughter, then tears, then anything we want
—I will put down my wine & be drunk on sorrow
—patrix: the male cradle of becoming through mind alone
—Freud's patient afraid she would disintegrate if anyone had her signature

This kind of collection makes me realize how life is a universe of fragments yearning for coherence. The intrinsic electricity I feel in this collection results from the diversity of the fragments and their longing to enter into conversation with one another. When I really sit down to write, I do not start with an empty page. Instead, I take out my notebook to sip from the many flavors clustered there. Or I comb through a half dozen notebooks for some constellation of points that might collectively plot a story, an essay, a speech. The *matrix,* or cradle of my experience in writing, is thus the constellation of gifts from the world, where I would have to invent the word *patrix* (reaching forward from my notebook entry) to identify invented wisdom that comes from mind alone. The patrix spins too weak a thread for me.

My high school English teacher—a marvel named Scholastica Murty—invited us to keep journals, and she issued us nicely bound blank books. After a decade in that habit, I found the standard, book-sized journal bulky and ostentatious—both in size and in my habit of filling them with my emotions. Working with others, in crowded, noisy rooms, I now like a journal the size of a grocery list, and I like finding my work in the words of people around me. I like smuggling stray thoughts into my notebook constantly. If anyone has influenced my practice directly, it may be Dorothy Wordsworth, whose Alfoxden and other journals show the power of detailed, external observations to convey interior experience. She demonstrates the power of listening with your whole body to what happens around you.

3. THE POSTCARD

What follows the tiny notebook entry? In another free moment, the postcard to yourself may be the right urge for the next sliver of time. Sometimes on the computer, sometimes on a blank page, I do a little writing from a promising lead. Take five minutes now and then to revisit something from your notebook, some glimpse or phrase, and to jot second thoughts, associations, "unrelated" material that comes, for some reason of its own, to your mind. Fragments matured to the size of a postcard stay with me, nibbling at my mind in the background. The world is busy, but the mind tenacious. The writing life is all about faith in a fragment.

4. THE LETTER

Now talk to someone far away, a good listener. Take one of your postcards and tell this thing you care about to someone who cares about you. (Sometimes in class we make a list of good listeners— both alive and gone: people who want to know everything from you. The list does not need to be long to be useful.) Somewhere in this letter, the subject may begin to gather wisdom—a tender increment. One sentence does more than the others. Or a cluster of sentences begins to find new momentum. Copy this sentence or longer sequence from the letter into your notebook, then mail the letter. You and your friend are both ahead. Your friend's faith in you has advanced your faith in your own ideas.

5. THE GATHERING

That rich cluster born somewhere in your letter now wants to find affinities—those magnetic ideas and moments of recollection and oblique association all in the same realm. This beginning is hungry. This nugget is the author, and you the scribe. On a fresh page, when you have a moment, you might list affinities that come to mind: moments from your random autobiography that connect, other fragments from your notebook, recent discoveries and quandaries, moments of insight from the last twenty-four hours. And somewhere in this gathering, several phrases may nominate themselves as titles for the whole.

6. THE TITLE

I put this here in the sequence, but sometimes the title comes before any of the actual writing. Sometimes in your notebook you will title a moment, a departure, a discovery. The title establishes new territory, a realm that belongs to you. Or the title may be hiding in the writing you have done. See if you find it somewhere in the random notes on your gathering page. Is there a phrase, or a word used in a new way, or a compact sentence that could become your little door opening a new dimension of experience that it is now your privilege to explore?

Looking back, I find a bundle of titles here that might help us. So far, if I were to title what I am writing now, I might call it "Faith in a Fragment," "A Realm that Belongs to You," "This Beginning Is Hungry," "A Tender Increment." Each title would not only identify the piece we are writing here, but might also transform our sense of what it is. These clues to naming the developing subject tend to hide everywhere in the flow of the writing.

7. THE DRAFT

Take ten minutes. Twenty would be a luxury. Sometimes five is all you have. Put your title or your sentence cluster at the top of the page, put your notebook and your gathering page to the side, and start talking on paper. Ask questions. Tell stories. Take detours. Tell secrets. Whisper and sing. Revel in words and textures. Let your whole body mutter and shout in the words that come. In class, we call this freewriting. In your own realm, it is simply your writing. Good things gather: huckleberries and whiskey in one bite.

8. THE MUSICAL KEY

Right away, or when you next have time, read what you have written aloud. Aloud. There is a line in a fifteenth-century monastic rule that specifies: "No one shall read while others are trying to sleep." Reading then was always done aloud, for literature is musical thought. In your writing now, what sings? Which sentence or phrase has a rhythm that you find enticing, commanding, enlivening?

Then ask, "What do you know that you didn't write?" Write what you didn't write, but in the musical tone of the part that sings. And then keep going as long as you can.

9. EXPANSION AND THE SECOND GENIUS

In my experience, revision happens best when it can have the same fervency as first writing. We might call this principle "the second genius," a deeper discovery latent in the first draft. In the realm of the second genius, discoveries do not happen alone, but in the rich context of earlier writing. Effects are magnified. Single jewels find a place in the firmament. You delve, sift, stir, and dig deep in your new property for gold. Somewhere in the first draft lies an opportunity to make great discoveries by adding what fits, and then by cutting what doesn't match the richest additions. The second genius is the midlife crisis of your young draft—messy, touched by loss, full of new power.

Transformation is possible at every point. By the magnetic principle of your eccentric mind, you add episodes, sentences, words, and you take out episodes, sentences, words. You change the order of what remains. You fine-tune every sentence by the musical ear you are developing exactly for this piece. Adding, cutting, moving, and tuning—these are the possible moves in revision, all energized by the spirit of the second genius.

It's a tough truth that drafts often get worse in revision, before they get better. This is natural. The first genius had a shine that may be tarnished by revision. There is a clear lawn, then the messy digging that begins a garden, then the order of the garden when it flourishes. It takes time, but you keep going through the messy stage, encouraged by the memory of how writing led you to the first genius, which began with nothing. But the first writing was often too small, too thin. It was shorthand for the whole message. This is why the second genius—the totally new finding of rich association and connection—is so essential.

10. RESPONSE FROM A WRITING GROUP

Beyond the good listener, don't share anything until you know what you love in what you have written. For if you, the artist, know the essential and unshakable pleasure at the heart of your work, bad advice can't hurt you. Sharing something to which you don't feel deep and present loyalty, however, is a waste of time for everyone, and dangerous. For if you don't know this deep pleasure in your writing, even good advice can stunt your work and steal your pleasure.

Writing groups advance work in progress to the extent the writer holds a matured sense of a work's core of integrity. As my father said, "An artist is someone who decides, not someone who goes to another and says, 'Is this good?'" If you hear that question from your own lips, take your work back to your studio and find its heart of pleasure on your own.

One day, it is time for the child to leave home. To remain longer would reverse the principle of healthy growth. That day comes when the child is mature enough to go out into the world, and the parent has other things to do. In the terrifying words of Donald Graves, we should not linger so long with a piece of writing that we begin "giving a manicure to a corpse." In my own practice, the end of revision may be accompanied by the abrupt sensation I am reading a piece written by someone much smarter than I am; a percussive click to the last line; or a flood of tears.

The bread is done when you can smell it from the next room. And your writing will get sassy, speak for itself, take on a life of its own you must not injure by meddling too long.

12. QUILT BLOCKS

A piece is finished. It is ready to escape you. Maybe it is the size of a poem, or a paragraph destined to be a paragraph alone. Maybe it is the size of a story of five hundred words, complete. Maybe it is a story that is complete in itself, but wants to be with other stories. Maybe it is a completed episode that wants to be part of a novel. Whatever the size of the completed piece, it came into being during a series of short time segments, twenty minutes or less, and the building of a larger structure—a book of poems, a collection of essays, an episodic nonfiction book, or a novel—can be constructed from quilt blocks of roughly the same magnitude as you accumulate them over time.

If this weren't true, I couldn't write in the midst of a busy life, and you could call me hypocrite to teach writing to students who are not independently wealthy and in possession of unlimited writing time. You're busy, I'm busy, we're in the same boat here. How do we move beyond the construction of small units of writing that satisfy us locally? As a first step, let's publish the pieces we have completed—the stories, poems, and essays—and simultaneously move to a consideration of compiling the larger work.

But first, before we follow that path to the end, let me pause a moment and test the first nine steps of my plan by writing a story to see what happens.

FREEDOM:

What has reached my hearing recently? That meeting with the lawyer? Too painful. Any dreams that lasted? Guess not. Something about that autumn maple tree outside, more vivid than ever, a kind of fire? Sounds hackneyed. Any recent learning from my teaching? Yeah, but I've already started to write about that. Wait: that story my mother told me, about the leaf, and the man. Wasn't there something in the notebook about that?

THE NOTEBOOK:

Mother's story about the man who offered to pick a branch outside the library for her.

THE POSTCARD:

So there's this woman coming out of the library, and she picks up a leaf, and a man sees her do this and offers to pick her a whole branch, and he breaks one off the tree even though she doesn't want it.

THE LETTER:

Dear Perrin, Last night you spoke of your mother, her creative spirit. A new understanding of my own mother starts when I remember a story she told me last week. All through her volunteer shift at the library, she kept glancing out the window at the sweet-gum tree in the parking lot, how stunning it was in its fall colors. As she left, she bent down to pick up a leaf, and a man who happened to be walking by offered to pick her a whole branch. She told him no thank you, but he started to break off a branch anyway, and it splintered, and he said he wished he had a knife, and then he tore it free and handed it to her.

My dear mother tells me these stories that have such truth in them it makes me afraid. One wants to give her things. She is such a generous person. But there is a danger somehow. When I mended your chair instead of writing Sunday, was that a selfish act? I write this note now to remind myself to ask you this tonight. See you then, Kim

THE GATHERING:

Okay, sit down to ramble freely: Colors of the sweetgum tree, the tree my mother calls "liquid amber." Is that a real name for it, or one she made up? What was that book from her day, *Forever Amber*? So, the man pulls off a branch and hands it to her. She is holding a leaf. Should she take the branch? Can she take it? How big is it? How big a branch could she hold with her one good hand? All through my growing up, her one hand seemed the normal way for a mother to be. Other mothers seemed like monsters, with two good hands that could grab you. My mother, holding out her left hand, seemed the way one should be: beckoning, welcoming, offering. What is it like for her this fall, two years after my father's death? My birthday, and my wife's in this season. Also the time of my brother's death. He was torn out of our family so suddenly. Daddy's death was different—sudden, but more natural, after a long life.

But my older brother, now somehow younger, gone. A branch of the family torn away.

THE TITLE:

Liquid Amber? A Leaf of Liquid Amber? Torn Away. Two Years After. A Story My Mother Told Me. A Branch of the Family. One Hand. A Leaf, a Hand.

THE DRAFT:

A Leaf, a Hand

"Wouldn't you like a whole branch?" The older man was beckoning to her.

"No, just this one leaf is enough." In her left hand, she held an autumn leaf. She had been looking out the office window all day at the young tree. When she started home, she had picked up one of the fallen leaves.

"Thank you for offering," she said.

"I'll just get you this twig," said the man. He was reaching up into the tree. The wood was brittle, and as he pulled on the twig, the whole branch split away.

"Oh," she said. "Please don't bother." The man was pulling on the branch, twisting it in the socket of wood, which was tearing.

"I always wanted a Swiss Army knife," said the man. "They're sharp, you know. Maybe I should just go get myself one." He continued to twist the branch. The man was puffing. As she glanced at him, his face was turning red. She hoped he would not have a heart attack.

The man was holding out the branch in both his hands.

"Oh," said the woman. "Please. I can't take that." She could not look at him. She could not say another word. Awkwardly, she turned away. He held the branch in his hands as she walked away holding her one leaf like a flame.

THE MUSICAL KEY:

I hear two rhythms in this story. One is the woman: "just this one leaf is enough." A cautious hesitation. The other is the man: "I always wanted a Swiss Army knife." Active. The meeting is an encounter between two rhythms. And what else? This story reminds me of Kawabata's *Palm-of-the-Hand Stories,* those prose vignettes of crucial episodes gleaned from many lives. In revision, I might focus on a few key tones—the color of the leaf, the gesture of the hand, the man's blindness to what the woman wishes. The tone of the piece is the absence of my father, my brother, those civilizing influences that protected my mother—and me—from the direct demands of this world. This story is actually about how I live my life, not my mother her life. As in a dream, I use a character based on her to understand my own predicament. I am caught in this life, this complex harmonic bell. This piece rings that bell.

EXPANSION:

A Leaf, a Hand

"Wouldn't you like a whole branch?" The nice-looking older man was beckoning to her.

"No, just this one leaf is enough." In her left hand, as if the fingers held a pencil, she thrust out an autumn leaf of the sweet-gum tree, flamed with red and yellow. She had been looking out the office window all day at the young tree. Every morning when she arrived, she would look. This was the first year it had shown the fullness of color more characteristic of an older tree. When she started home, she had picked up one of the fallen leaves.

"Thank you for offering," she said. She had seen the man before. He sometimes walked by as she was leaving work. The season was beginning to be chilly. It was dusk now, when she started home.

"I'll just get you this twig," said the man. He was reaching up into the tree toward a branch that seemed to be on fire. The wood was brittle, and as he tugged on the twig, the whole branch split away.

"Oh," she said. "Please. Don't." The man was pulling on the branch, twisting it in the socket of wood, which was tearing.

"I always wanted a Swiss Army knife," said the man as he struggled. "They're sharp, you know. Maybe I should just go get myself one." He continued to twist the branch. Faces had appeared in the office window. A car, leaving the parking lot, had paused. Its windows reflected the colors of the tree, trembling now. The woman looked at the ground. A breeze made the fallen leaves twitch. She had taken the best one. The others each had some flaw. The man was puffing. As she glanced at him, his face was turning red. She hoped he would not have a heart attack.

"Guess I'll give you a bigger gift than I meant to." The man gave a mighty tug, and with a shudder, the tree released both the branch and a ribbon of bark. The bark peeling off the tree sounded like a long zipper opening. The woman looked at the deep scar on the trunk of the sapling, and the white wood inside, glistening. The man was holding out the branch in both his gloved hands. The gloves were new. He must have treated himself to new gloves, early in the season, before the real cold.

"Oh," said the woman. "Please. I can't take that." She could not look at him. She could not say another word. Awkwardly, she turned away.

"I can break you off a smaller part," he said to her back, "for in a vase, maybe." The woman, walking away, was getting smaller. He took a few steps after her, dragging the branch on the sidewalk. The woman was hurrying now, getting even smaller at the corner. Just before she disappeared, he saw the right sleeve of her coat swinging loose. His own right arm went numb.

That's it. But what happened? In expansion, in my search for the story's second genius, the story changed. Although the writing began with my mother's story, I see it is no longer about my mother, but about my own feeling of dislocation following my brother's death, and then my father's. I am the woman in the story, and also the man. There is no way to take the big gift—to bring my father back, or my brother. There is only this little story, this one leaf. The world plucks life away, branch by branch. Maybe I can grow my own tree, leaf by leaf, story by story.

Now I have made this block from my little solitudes. This little story—what is it? And where do I go from here?

Perhaps because of my habit of broad hospitality in the notebook—where I gather rich fragments—the books in process on my desk now are each based in some kind of honeycomb structure that will welcome these fragments. My novel consists of fifty interconnected monologues. My essay collection I call "Eight American Journeys," eight cells for collecting local jewels from the world. Poems often begin with a line from the notebook that has a heartbeat in it, a particular rhythm and warmth that wants to stay small, and then the poems gather into a sequence of their own. And speeches often begin with a phrase—"a midsummer night's dream for Oregon"—

and follow with a series of compact local discoveries that have appeared recently in my notebooks.

What if I want to write a long piece structured by a single, evolving idea, a formal piece of exposition? I did that once, a 316-page dissertation designed to fit a schema not native to my daily experience. The task earned me a degree, but did not feel honest. As my advisor put it, "Yours may be the most turgid prose ever penned." And I believe it was. It was a dense, and unwavering pursuit of proof, a predatory dinosaur. Writing it, I experienced a kind of exclusive concentration that wounded me. I survived by occasionally pushing aside a volume of medieval scholarship to jot stray lyric impulses on the three-by-five-inch bibliography cards in my pocket, which then became folded and gathered sheets of typing paper as I neared the end, and later evolved into the pocket notebooks I now sew together a half a dozen at a time.

How does a larger work develop from the compact piece? How do we piece the quilt, now that the individual blocks can be made in the time we have?

It struck me during a faculty meeting recently that we might have been given insights sudden and grand. Life could be a sustained burst of light—or darkness. Instead we are given nights punctuated by days, and days punctuated by nights. We tend to receive glimmerings, hints, occasional fragments, and quiet insights. We live a sequence of limited sensations threaded by time into a longer curve of developing experience. This is why we are required to honor small moments of learning, to have faith in fragments, and over time to quilt our solitudes into whole structures.

13. WHERE TO PUBLISH THESE PIECES

The first stages of my experiment, then, are over. Here is a story, "A Leaf, a Hand," a single page. And you will have stories of your own you have lived with longer than I with mine. You give them time, tinker, seek for each a further genius inside this scaffold of the early draft. But then, my friends, what shall we do with our stories?

In my experience it works this way: You go to the library. Or you go to the magazine store, a good one, like Rich's Cigar Store in Portland. You survey the literary holdings there—*Fireweed, Prairie Schooner, Glimmer Train, Shenandoah, Mud City Review.* Which hospitable issues catch your eye? You take them down, look at many, buy a few. You share your favorites with friends. You may cheat, and resort to some compendium like *Writer's Market,* or the *Writer's Northwest Handbook,* and these can be useful, but you will want to hold the actual journals in your hands, to read them through. If you were published in this one, would you be in good company? The answer must be yes. You make a list of magazines that make you feel this yes. You start local, with magazines in your own community, state, region. Maybe you subscribe, or get your local library to subscribe. If the magazine isn't good enough to tempt you to subscribe, what does this say about your desire to be published there?

14. HOW TO PUBLISH THESE PIECES

Out of the solitudes available to you, over the length of time necessary, you have sixteen or twenty poems, you have a dozen stories, you have six or eight essays. You need a full set, for it is too dangerous to your ego, and too hard in practice to start a sustained conversation with an editor by trying to publish the one story, the one poem, the one essay you have written. Rejection often accompanies single submissions; editorial conversation and eventual acceptance for publication accompany successive submissions over time.

Using information you gleaned from the small print in the magazines you admire (editors' names and addresses, appropriate forms and seasons of submission), you now set up a sequence that can be automatic: You submit, and if a piece is returned by one magazine, it goes out the next day to the next magazine in your rotation of favorites. Perhaps five sets of four poems work the rotation of half a dozen magazines one by one. A dozen stories may work the rotation of a dozen magazines. When your pieces are returned, strive for one-day turnaround. If a returned piece comes with an encouraging note, you have a sequence of additional pieces to send directly to that editor of taste.

You need to keep finished pieces off your desk, or the temptation to endlessly revise and perhaps ruin them will distract you from your current work with new material. That is the one thing you can't afford, because your work now relies completely on the short segments of solitude available to you. Don't submit work you don't feel is finished; don't revise work that is finished. Keep the lines clear, and strive for continuity of process within the time you have.

At a party, when someone asks what you do, don't say, "I'm a writer." People are kind, they try to make conversation, and you won't yet have anything to say when they ask, "Oh, you're a writer? What have you published?" Use the verb, not the noun: "I've been doing some writing."

"Oh, what have you been writing?"

"Well, I have this little piece I love called 'Quilting Your Solitudes.' I don't quite know what it is yet, but it's growing on me."

Quilting Your Little Solitudes into a Book

Now you are writing regularly within the time you have, and as you go, you are submitting pieces that please you. That sequence has become automatic, like piano chords played by the left hand. Now for the overarching melody: How do these little pieces that please you add up to a whole book?

Gathering poems is easy. You write a poem a day—or a poem a week, or a poem a month, or even a poem a year—and eventually they add up to a collection you shuffle into order, title, and submit to a publisher who publishes other poets you admire (again starting local in your search for a worthy publisher, then regional, and working outward). But what about a novel, or a series of substantial essays, or a nonfiction book? How does such a grand project get written, and compiled, in the limited arena of your little solitudes?

Let me mention six books that may serve as models, each constructed of small pieces that appear to have been independently created, but that add up to a whole work. In each, the title and related conception of genre are essential liberating tools in construction.

1. Barry Lopez, *Field Notes* (New York: Knopf, 1994)

Reading these concise and evocative stories, I'm instructed by the practical advantage of the title. "Stories" are one thing, "Field Notes" quite another. Don't these notes, these imaginings, these parables have great freedom because of the way the writer has identified them? Lopez has used a title that gives him great permission to gather richly disparate things and deliver them to a reader in attractive form.

2. Dorothy Allison, *Two or Three Things I Know for Sure* (New York: Plume, 1995)

Again the title makes a particular, limited claim that results in broad permission. Allison gathers a series of autobiographical vignettes and family photographs around two prevailing questions: Within a family, what do men do to women, and what do women do for each other? The result is a collective family portrait that reads like a novel, and like a study of our kind, and also like nothing ever made before. The concise claim of the title—the defining range of "two or three things I know"—enables Allison to explore a generous chronological and thematic territory without getting lost. Small claim, big territory, and a compass of informing questions in the hand.

3. David James Duncan, *River Teeth* (New York: Doubleday, 1995)

In his introduction, Duncan explains that "river teeth" are the little icons of wood whittled out of fallen trees by the abrasive action of rivers—the enduring knots of greatest density. This named idea enables Duncan to gather a series of "tales" and "epiphanies" into a cohesive sequence. They are short. They are dense. They have survived in the mind by the tenacity of their importance. And now they want to be together. What is this book—fiction? Yes. Memoir? Yes. And it reads like, well—like river teeth.

4. Kathleen Dean Moore, *Riverwalking*

(New York: Lyons and Burford, 1995)

The chapters in this book consist of clusters of story and reflection associated with a series of named rivers. The first chapter, for example, weaves several nonfiction paragraphs through a narrative about a family camping trip on the Willamette River. In this chapter, some of the nonfiction paragraphs begin:

> "My daughter comes from a long line of people with strong homing instincts."
> "When I was first married . . ."
> "I know a biologist who studies the homing instincts of garter snakes."
> "Scientists say that a wasp can leave its hole in the ground."

And so on, deft little essays sidling through a more direct narrative about a particular camping trip. Moore thus brings together the compact essays of a paragraph or two in length with narratives of place. Collectively, these form chapters of a dozen pages, which then are joined by the simple principle of chapters named for rivers to form a whole book.

If a writer does not have an uncluttered year to write, it is possible thus to write in a series of short bursts and let the engine of the book's idea do the work of collecting these pieces into a whole.

5. Doris Grumbach, *Fifty Days of Solitude*
   (Boston: Beacon Press, 1994)
   Grumbach begins with a thought from Conrad's *Heart of Darkness:* "We live, as we dream—alone." She then compiles a sequence of observations, recollections, and discoveries that came to her in the course of a fifty-day stretch of isolation in a house on the Maine coast. This book came from a sustained stretch of time, but it could have been written in a series of smaller solitudes stretched out over as long as it took to complete them. Grumbach's book reminds me it is not my life that limits my writing, but my understanding of the miniature opportunities resident in my life. Conditions will not change soon, but I can still make progress by developing my writing plan in keeping with current conditions.

6. Theodore Roethke, *Straw for the Fire,* selected and arranged by
   David Wagoner (Garden City, N.Y.: Doubleday, 1972)
   Roethke's mature method of composing poems consisted largely of writing individual, self-contained lines of poetry, and then gathering these lines into poems. Wagoner here presents unconnected sequences of Roethke's independent lines, taken directly from his notebooks, so we may experience the power of the independent thought, and the musical possibilities Roethke had available when he sat down to weave his single threads into mesmerizing poems.

Lopez, Allison, Duncan, Moore, Grumbach, and Roethke each provide a mosaic of glimpses housed in a work that hefts as a book. Little pieces, governed by some intrinsic pattern of order, become extended vehicles for understanding.

So, my friends, how shall we do this now? Each block in the quilt glows bright in its color, and each is held fast in the quilted whole. Piece by piece, you find the tiny key that is without weight or substance, the trick of beginning, a key as small as the syllables "Open Sesame!" This is available to each of us. How long is a writer's effective solitude? How much time does it take to do the whole work? In all the darkness of the world, to strike one match is enough to begin. The rest is step by step, light by little light, until your book is made, and then it lets you go, and there it stands: field notes, river teeth, a few things I know for sure, or this project I have called "Quilting Your Solitudes."

My father was fond of quoting from Nietzsche, as I remember it, "In our time of doubt about all 'certainties,' sustained intellectual discourse is hypocrisy." Maybe my father liked that because he had four children who made it difficult for him to enter the long trance of writing sustained discourse. He wrote compact poems before first light, and threaded them together into collections. I write sequences of short meditations and lyric stories pieced into quiltlike essays and fictional works. And the artesian source of it all is this trove of fragments in the tiny book I carry. If the house catches fire, if I ever die, my greatest treasure now is already in my pocket.

Years ago, in the closing session of a yearlong class, as we each shared our life plan for ongoing creation, one woman said simply, "I plan to eat well, and see what happens." So we feed on words, questions, stories. Dear students, friends, let's try this way of feasting on the language, keeping a notebook, quilting solitudes, and seeing what happens.

LOOKING FOR MR. NU

When I conducted a writing workshop in Port Angeles, Washington, someone asked, "How do you write an essay?" That was our topic, and I was the visiting expert hired to know. But somehow the question stalled me. I couldn't explain. We went around the table and told something of ourselves (the introductions becoming longer and more interesting stories as we went). Then that question again, "How *do* you write an essay?" All I could do was to say something about working from a sense of abundance. "Abundant what?" they asked. Well, that's what we don't know yet. Once we know, each of us, then we can begin writing essays. My guess is that the process of writing essays may be less a matter of physically writing—scrabbling with paper and ink—and more a matter of living toward some kind of dense mystery. You get the abundance by living, and find the coherence by writing.

We spent the day writing short fragments from various tendrils of our experience, reaching forward from the stories by which we had introduced ourselves, toward secrets we were ready to tell. In the midst of it all, as I watched them work, their questions about the essay made me realize I think of myself as more capable of listening than of saying, at first—listening to the muttering of my own mind, and also to neighbors at the café counter, fellow travelers at the bus station, dreams, memories, words in the air all around us all the time. When do notes become essays? As the words in the air intensify to the level of barrage, something comes together. But the knit of thought comes seldom fast, rarely soon, almost never in fully recognizable form in the space of a workshop day. You have to go forth and ponder.

At the writing workshop, though, everyone around the table had something lucky: one with nine children, another with no children and a vagabond life of yearning. One with a knowledge of biology and a hunger for something else. One with family stories that no one tells outside the family. Confusion is a rich source, I said. You can write from that, if you pay close attention, coax a speaking voice out from the snarl of it. Really good sorrow has served me well sometimes, I said. They looked at me.

We all wanted the writing to be possible: Climb into a canoe, and set out. But what was the canoe, and how could we load it with our joys and sorrows? Our experience was so big, it would not fit to the small passage of word by word.

We wrote together, searching for stories from our lives. We talked, searched, took some hints to heart, and then the workshop came to an end.

Driving south for home that night, I puzzled it through. How *do* you write an essay? The world should answer that, not the teacher. I knew, as I traveled, for me the floating bridge was part of it, strung out light by light across the strait. And the water was part of it, a restless shoreline all along Puget Sound. I stopped to sort through the driftwood above the sand: a whole forest whittled into pieces and strewn there by waves. I picked up a few sticks to take along, tied one to the top of my car. South from Quilcene, I stood by the trees to chill myself awake, the whole trees standing on the mountain with me. Time had not yet taken them apart. I wanted to inhale the long line of their shadows, the pelt of their darkness. Then on.

Somewhere south of Shelton, I had to doze. Pulled off on a dirt road where the power lines ran, rolled out my bag in the back of the car, and slept. Once in the night I woke to the bright beam of a state trooper's light shining in on me.

"I conked out driving home from Port Angeles," I said through the open window.

"And what's this long stick tied to your car?"

"I don't know," I said, "I just found it and thought I could use it to get kites out of trees." He studied my face a few moments in the beam.

"Okay," he said, "sorry to wake you." He snapped off his light, trudged back to his car, and sped away.

I drifted off to sleep, but woke often to hear the tapered growl of trucks carrying their loads north, or south. A road gives two choices. That's not enough.

The next morning, off on a country road, I stood on the main street in the town of Bucoda peering through the cracked window of the junk shop into a rusted mound of tools, paintings, furniture, and dust. Two enormous locks held the hasp at the door, and inside, electric wires bristled from the knob. Above the door, a message to the world in red spray paint made the wall shine: LOCKS ELECTRICALLY CHARGED. Then I saw the handwritten letter taped to the glass from inside:

> The passing of a loving and dear friend. Now I'm not married so its not my wife But mans best friend "His Dog." My dog Bandito

part husky disappeared from my home in Bucoda Friday Jan 3rd 1985. A neighbor reported that he heard a gun shot which woke him up 4 PM Saturday morning I hope you Bandito didn't die of a gun shot wound. I hear you were taken by force that you leave a house of good master a nice and loving. Im beginning to miss your presence at foot of my bed when I eat a meal your beging for a share that Im having Im glad that I had a part of your life you will be missed.

> signed a old man of
> Bucoda Wash
> Mr. Nu

And then I was driving over the mountain south, past the gaping coal pit two miles across, where giant trucks crawled up the spiral mud road to carry carbon rock to the plant erupting with steam, then down along cutover land, stump farms, soggy winter towns, the river burrowing through pastures, until I came to a barn with a good roof. The sign—"Antiques"—gave me permission to study the building from inside. And there was Dude, who ran the place with her bustling good humor. She straightened from her work on a weathered hutch and gestured with a wire brush.

"Wander through all three floors and take your time, but just remember to always shut the doors behind you as you go."

I went winding up stairways past the maple school desks and purple glass kerosene lamps, the saw vise, rag rug, loom parts in a heap, clear up to the narrow room at the top where a plain white blanket folded on a bench took my hand into its wool folds, held me by the fingers, unwrapped itself on the bed so I could see its handspun overall pure glory. The selvage was worn, soft to the finger, and the one red weft band of pattern almost fit where the two loom-widths of the cloth were sewn together, like two old lovers sleeping side by side.

Someone had pinned a crumpled note to the blanket at the corner:

These 2 pieces of wool belonged to my Grandmother Bohn. She raised the sheep—washed & carded—then made yarn and wove this material. This must have been in the middle of the eighteen hundreds—maybe 1860–70. Freda.

I folded the blanket under my arm. Stood awhile by the window. Soft weather of rain through a cracked pane of glass.

"Ah," said Dude, when I came down, "the blanket. You found it! Sir, this will sound chauvinistic, but, for a man, you have good taste. Did you see the note? Of course. I don't see how anyone could sell that out of the family. One of my pickers bought it from another picker who brought it up from Oregon. Can you imagine selling a thing like that out of the family? No! I kept it in the closet for several years myself, couldn't stand to offer it for sale. I'd take it out and show it to special people. It's the kind of thing that doesn't seem part of money. Doesn't belong in a store. I had it in the closet. Then one day I said to myself, 'This is ridiculous.' So I brought it to the barn, put it way upstairs. And now you've found it. I'll let it go. Take care of it. Yes?"

On down the little back roads I drove, with my hand on the blanket beside me. I followed the land, valley to valley, where the narrow highway obeyed bigger rivers, turned aside for fencerows, zigzagged around the corners of farms older than asphalt. In Kalama, in another secondhand store, I talked to McCoy Loony, proprietor of amber beads, loggers' steel tools, wax flowers, Indian stone bowls, and old words sliding smooth off his tongue.

"What's that stick cross on the wall?" I said.

"Logger art," he said. "No, tramp art. The loggers learned it from the tramps. Tramp could take a walnut shell, sit around drilling little holes in it with a knife—never used more than a pocket knife—and put in twigs for feet, something to swivel for a head, and a little bitty stick tail. Set that on the sidewalk and wait for the kids to come by. You see, the head and tail, they moved. Something made them move like something alive. Sold that for two bucks to them kids. Kids made their parents buy them just to see what made it work. Bought it, opened the walnut shell, and a big old horsefly flew off. Had that fly trapped in there to bump the sticks and wag the tail, wobble the head. But then it was just two halves of a walnut shell and the sticks. No life left. Those tramps!"

"What about the stick cross?"

"Finn fellow made that—from Long Beach, maybe. Here on the coast." And Mr. Loony took it down for me: hundreds of whittled sticks of fir sapwood puzzled interlocking into a cross. In my hands, it flexed, every whittled facet of the wood saying something about patience, interdependence, silence of the one spirit, time spent alone with the hands at work.

"Won't find too many like that now," said Mr. Loony.

"Coy," his wife called from the back room, "you selling that cross?"

"Looks like." Coy looked at me, spit in the ashtray and stubbed his cigarette with a hiss. "There's one little piece in all that now," he said, "you have to watch for. If that one piece comes loose, the whole thing will just unravel to nothing. Pile of sticks again. I've looked for that key pin, but never could find it."

The blanket and the cross on the seat beside me now, I drove south for Oregon. How do you write an essay? I added the figures in my mind. The cost of the blanket and of the cross almost exactly equaled my pay for the workshop on how to write an essay. I had two dollars to spare, so I stopped in Woodland for coffee, to spend it all clean and think this clear.

Fitting my elbows to the twin worn spots on the Formica counter, stirring my bitter coffee just to hear the spoon ring, I began: There is a blanket, there is a cross. There is Dude and Coy. There is the grandmother weaving, and the old Finn whittling. There is woman and man, their hands working wool and wood. There is the design of the spirit cross, and there is the long cold life that makes the body need. And there is Mr. Nu.

My two hands closed around my cup. How do you save life? You start with wool, a fleece taken whole off the ewe in spring. Or you start with a block of old-growth fir, even-grained, fragrant in hand. You start by taking this whole thing apart—picking and carding and spinning the fleece, splitting and shaving and trimming the wood, working it down to a strand of wool, a bundle of splinters long and even. Then you put it back together, the beater of the loom bumping thread on thread, and the old Finn's fingers sliding each wood spline into its own locked place. You start with the words of a letter to the world, about an old dog loved, and you find what wants to go with that.

At the counter it came to me I don't much whittle, and I don't weave lately. Mostly now, I write. I take the seamless rush of my days and tease out the hum of the road, the rim shadow of mountains, the trooper's blaze of curiosity, the words of Mr. Nu. If this were an essay now, would I call it "Dude and Coy"? Would I call it "The Blanket and the Cross"? Would I call it "Best Friend"? Or maybe "Looking for Mr. Nu." I must go look for Mr. Nu. Maybe he will tell me a story no one has ever heard. Something was ripped from the center of his life. The open-pit mine on the back road is one kind of hurt, and the chasm in the heart of Mr. Nu another. Could the blanket or the cross heal that? Could the telling of his own story heal that? That's my research. I must try to thread the pieces back together as I follow this road, as I fold this blanket, as I flex this cross, and as I knit this essay snug for you.

Happy Problems

Most of a writer's difficulties are what my father used to call "happy problems." I remember hearing this phrase often as a cheerful response to my report of anguish. Childhood is so rich with possibilities, we kids often experienced summer afternoon as a crisis: Should we swim, hike to the local forest, make a fort in the yard, shoot bows and arrows, or call a friend? We viewed these choices as conflicting claims; our father viewed them as rich options. Now my father is gone, and I am left with his philosophic challenge: happy problems. As writers we have plenty.

Writers need to embrace the whole opportunity of writing, especially the "hard" parts, and say, like the friar in *Romeo and Juliet,* in the midst of great distress, "There art thou happy." Writing is difficult work, but it is your privilege to have the treasure of the language ready. There art thou happy. True originality is elusive, but no one experiences the world quite as you do. There art thou happy. No one can really help you, but this isolation may make the best of your quiet self bold. There art thou happy.

For a writer, happy problems reside in the lucky hardship of finding ways to do what no one has ever done. To be original, one must embrace happy problems: all this feeling, all this memory, all these ways I could say what I almost know.

The Happy Problem of Originality

It gives me uncommon joy to come across rich originality in an unexpected place, like this single, Shakespearean sentence in the *Audubon Society Field Guide to North American Wildflowers* by Richard Spellenberg (New York: Knopf, 1979):

> After the summer heat dries the low mountains, driving most wildflowers to seed and browning the grasses, Red Shrubby Penstemon begins to flower, providing a final source of nectar before the hummingbirds must seek food higher in the cooler mountains or, if late in the season, migrate south.

Can facts ever be original? Alone, no. But a new connection among a constellation of dispersed facts is always original. There lies the pleasure of discovery and creation.

Let's say you and I have felt the despairing sense that everything has already been said. Then comes the moment when we realize that precedent is one of many muses. If you go into the material as yourself, you will find an original way. Haven't we all heard that derivative but highly original country song:

> Blame it on your lyin', cheatin', cold dead-beatin',
> two-timin', double-dealin', mean mistreatin', lovin' heart.

Once that line is before us, we realize it waited a long time to be discovered. It took an omnivorous look at old materials for a writer unafraid to create a completely new song.

When you set out to create a fictional world, your most startling effects may be the rearrangement of known elements. I take my cue from the news. If I were making not a story or poem, but a new nation, how could I be most original? I want to be as creative as these diplomats: A breakaway former Soviet republic, Abkhazia, as one of its first official acts printed a postage stamp filled with the grinning faces of Marx and "Lenin"—in this case Groucho Marx and John Lennon. In one stroke, despite their great difficulties ahead, they expressed a break with history, a love of art, a tie to the West, and a sense of humor. This makes me wonder what moves in my own writing could catch that kind of verve and originality.

We are talking about improvisation here—knowing an old tune (Marx and Lenin), but not quite playing it as it has been played before —at all. In some ways, the more familiar the material, the more stunning the creative shift may be.

A friend writes me to describe a Cherokee game called Flip the Coined Phrase. It seems that part of Cherokee culture is pleasure in linguistic stunts, a game of verbal gymnastics—conducted with both close friends and ardent enemies. The game goes like this: Start with a common phrase, and begin to juggle the words in all ways. The cliché "Talk is cheap" soon becomes "Talk is cheap, but good conversation is priceless." Or "Talk is cheap, until you dial long distance." You might begin with "I love you" and travel past "Why do I love you" to "How do I love thee, let me count the ways" and "It's a miracle I still love you" and "It's a wonder I love you despite your faults" to arrive finally at "The wonder is not that I love you despite your faults; the miracle is that I love you despite *my* faults."

The writer says something new by listening to the cliché as if listening to a "problem student": Somewhere inside that soul lies great wisdom. How to tease it forth? The poet Charles Simic once wrote, "The dream of every honest cliché is to enter a great poem." Yes. The happiness of this process makes me giddy. I want to say to the language: Give me your tired, your stale, your deadened words yearning to breathe free, and I will make them citizens in the new land.

Like a discouraged writer, a teacher might have the feeling that everything has already been taught. But even here lies a bonus. Going to class, meeting a new group of students, I need to be totally original by making the most of all my most recent learning. And I need every member of the class to help.

Coming into class, I might begin, "Hey, you all, I just overheard Christy say . . . and did anyone see that line of graffiti outside? . . . and by the way, what have you been reading? . . . has anyone written something recently that puzzled them? . . . listen to this letter I just received . . . it occurred to me . . . what did you notice on your way to class? . . . who is stuck on a piece of writing? Really? Let's talk about that."

I find with these questions and oblique nudges that my teaching style reflects my experience as a writer. New ideas do not come from nowhere. Rather, a seed in recent and seemingly ordinary experience may quicken a train of original ideas *as if* from nowhere. The search for originality is not a struggle but a realm of play. As Oscar Wilde said, "Life is too important to be taken seriously." Time is short, the stakes are high, and our only option is spirited and playful exploration. As a writer, I find myself faced often by this lucky desperation: in a busy day, with only five minutes to write, what's fresh in my notebook, most new and strange? The writing of an essay on my life journey through music began with a piece of graffiti a student first reported:

To do is to be.
—Camus

To be is to do.
—Sartre

Do-be-do-be-do.
—Sinatra

The Happy Problem of Secrecy

Some things are too private to tell. Some of our best stories are family secrets. We might hurt others by telling them, we say. It's not our place to reveal them, we say. And yet secrets are also what we long to tell. It seems to me that we should write secrets we are *ready* to tell. If our stories are not in some way secret, they are not very interesting. And if they are secrets we are not yet ready to tell, we shouldn't tell them. But the boundary seems to shift daily between secrets we are not ready to tell and those we are. Yesterday, this was too private. Today, it's ready. Tomorrow, it may seem ordinary.

My father wrote every day for some fifty years. And yet, a month before he died, I asked him some tough questions, and he told me things I don't believe he had ever told anyone. Though he seemed in good health that summer of 1993, for some reason I was moved to sit down with my father and grill him: "What ever happened to your father? What was it like when you came back home, a pacifist, after World War II? And what about your mother—how was it for her after your father died?"

"She'd been left at the poor farm," he said. "No one came. There was no one there who knew her. When I got there, she looked at me. 'Billy,' she said, 'you have to get me out of here.' And I wanted to say, 'Of course I'll get you out of here.' But I didn't know if I could."

And then something happened I had never seen. My father cried. Quietly, without moving. His big fist was still on the table.

I put my hand on my father's hand. He didn't move, stared straight ahead. He, the writer every day for fifty years, had never told this moment that gripped him so. He looked at me. A week later, he was gone.

The Happy Problem of Form

Often, when a piece of writing begins, we don't know what it is. This is inefficient. This is probably unprofessional. And this is unavoidable, if we want to live by happy problems. For the discovery of form from the originating vantage point of unruly content is happy hunting. What does a given fragment of experience *want* to be?

In the middle of a film, it strikes me that the close-up on a big screen—a face ten feet tall—makes any cinematic story psychological, and returns us to that time in childhood when proportion felt out of control.

What to do with that quirky thought? Is it an essay, the beginning of a movie review, a poem that gives the film version of a moment from childhood? Or is that part of a conversation inside a short story? If the answer is "story," then is it a new story, or is this the perfect new element in a story I already have in progress?

These questions form our happiness as writers. For "happiness" in the original sense is simply "hap," events, "what happens." To be happy is to be in keeping with events unfolding around us. This is the Tao of the writing craft: Don't fight. Don't suffer. Be with.

The writer Kawabata ended his career by rewriting one of his novels, *Snow Country,* as a short story. He had to take that long path—from idea, to novel, to short story—to get the tale exactly right. In my own practice, essays were a mystery until I realized a letter with a title was my kind of essay. Letters were easy, essays were hard, until this bridge appeared. But without struggling with my teacher's version of "the essay," I might never have found my own.

One student told me, "I write about something in poetry because I don't know what to say about it in talk." Others use poems as rough drafts for essays, or glean favorite lines from prose journals to smuggle into poems. All this clumsy shuffling is exactly what we should be doing when we set out to learn the form a given episode of writing is trying to inhabit. A student once told our class, "I keep thinking I'm going to learn how to write short stories, but by the time I finish one, all I have learned is how to write *that* short story. I still don't know how to write short stories. I guess I'll just have to keep learning, story by story."

The Happy Problem of Confusion

"I just don't get it." Remember in school when you said that sentence to yourself in despair, or to a teacher in hope? As a writer now, I move sideways, try something oblique, bring in new material, start over with gusto. Not getting it means I must be doing original work. The feeling of not getting it is a good sign, not a paralyzing signal. The writing is hard because I am seeking connections that I did not know before—that nobody knew before. To proceed under such conditions is the hardest thing to do and the only thing worth doing.

The feeling of not getting it is like rain for the dry-land farmer—uncomfortable as you hunch on the tractor seat, but the best thing for the ground. This anxious feeling is the growing place. To be an expert—assured—is death to the process that creates expertise. For expertise comes from not knowing—yet.

I feel I am something of an expert on salutary confusion, having lived with it for years. My wife says I get quiet when I have something big coming up—a speech to give, a new class about to begin, an essay brewing. "If I didn't know you," she says, "you might seem depressed. But that's not it. You're gathering new stuff, that's all. You *need* to get nervous to do it the way you like."

The Happy Problem of Error

Sometimes a fertile source for invention is to hear something wrong, or read something wrong, or make a "false" connection in mind, and then to recognize the original creation you have just found. In the weaving studio, someone calls across the room, "Will you help me when I dye?" But, of course, in my hearing I spell that last word "wrong," and suddenly feel ready to write a story to contain the plea, "Will you help me when I die?"

Listening to country music, with the volume just a little too low, can bring gold. Those lines you almost hear, and have to make up to make out, belong to you. Of course, with country, you never know whether you heard a line or made it up, so familiar is the sweet realm of humor in sorrow:

Like butter on bread, she spreads her love around.

Did I invent that, or hear it? (For years I thought that was mine, but it was from my friend John Lane.) And classical music is not immune to such surprise. I once dozed fitfully through an entire live cantata, enjoying the lyric lines I half heard, only to learn during the applause that the entire text had been in German—the lines I "heard" in English I had invented: "Turn around and share my sleep." I had to feverishly try to write down the lines I got "wrong," because they belonged to me.

These minor examples point me in the direction of more profound "error" and greater magnitude of resulting discovery. As a child, for example, I apparently got several family stories wrong, lived with my own versions for forty years, and now stand in rich possession of personal myth: Jesus called my own relatives to fish a Nebraska lake during a great storm. I like that. And Uncle Miley, was he really struck by lightning after returning home on Valentine's Day from three years on the road? History happened. I write what I know, because my knowing is shaped by creative selection. "Error" may be the small door to the great realm: how we might live.

Buddha said and my father knew that life is suffering. But out of suffering and confusion may come creation. So go forth, and embrace your happy problems. Mystery and difficulty are your greatest fortune.

PERSONAL MEMORY AND FICTIONAL CHARACTER

For years I have gone to class unprepared to teach. Please don't tell my dean. I don't *want* to live this way, and I'm sometimes stricken with guilt. But the world is such a busy place, and the phone rings, the in-box fills with mail I feel I must answer, and I'm so optimistic about my ability to do it all that class time rolls around, and I haven't planned my lecture on how to write.

On second thought, though, maybe this inability is actually my greatest resource. Maybe you *should* tell my dean—that I have, by force of long practice, attained a Zenlike presence of mind when I walk into class "unprepared." In this trancelike state, *everything* becomes rich opportunity for teaching.

I remember a conversation I overheard between a faculty member and our writer in residence, Jim Heynen.

"I would consider it un*conscionable*," said the professor, "to begin a class session without complete preparation—an understood subject of inquiry and agreement on relevant texts considered well in advance."

"I would consider it un*conscionable*," Jim replied, "to begin class with such an established sense of subject and relevant resources that we would prevent the intuitive connections at the heart of true learning."

Of course the truth lies between these extremes, but I lean toward Jim's hunch. I remember my father saying that early in his teaching career he would ask himself at the beginning of each term, "Have I read enough to be a good teacher?" And he would have to answer, "No, not yet." Then one year, when he asked himself this question, he realized he could answer, "Yes, I have now read enough to be a good teacher." But then a different question presented itself: "Am I a good teacher?" And he had to answer, "No, I'm not—not always. For teaching is an art: Sometimes it works, and sometimes it doesn't."

Another time he said to me that the days he found himself carrying all kinds of readings and plans to class, he knew he wasn't prepared to teach. But when he approached class with nothing, except a question or two in which for some reason he felt great confidence, he was ready.

It often happens that thirty minutes before a three-hour graduate writing seminar is to begin, I am standing at my desk looking at the clutter before me with a wild hunter's total concentration: What from my current mail, from my recent reading or travel, or from the notebook in my pocket might form the basis for our time tonight? Almost always, I am overwhelmed with treasure. For I find I have been preparing nonstop since the last class, simply by absorbing the richest things I stumble upon. A lecture I attend, a story I read, a conversation I overhear, a quirky juxtaposition I observe, even a dream and a line from my own writing may braid their way into a sequence of writing and discussion activities we may productively try together. There may even be a short lecture in the mix, or what often feels like a sermon when I come to give it.

To test this more charitable interpretation of my teaching habits, I have typed up, as an exercise, the cluster of ideas, readings, and invitations I grabbed for a recent three-hour seminar at the Northwest Writing Institute. In the preceding week, my wife and I had attended a lecture by Kazuo Ishiguro; browsing in the library, I had been seduced by a book on Edward Hopper; nights I had been reading a biography of Emerson; my students' questions the previous week had me thinking about Carol Bly's *The Passionate, Accurate Story,* which I was bringing to class—and somehow all this led me to imagine a series of writing invitations sparked by an old idea from the writer H. E. Bates. As we sat down together, I asked the class (searching for an opening) if they had some recent questions suggested by the writing they had been doing. One said, yes, she was wondering what to do with some pieces she had written for a memoir class, now that she wanted to try fiction. This caused me to pull out my notebook and read to her what I had written following the lecture by Ishiguro, and we were on our way. Here is roughly how it went:

1. Kazuo Ishiguro talks about the "vacuum" surrounding certain fictional characters. They are defined by what they *don't* say, what they *don't* do. The most powerful thing about Spencer, the butler in *The Remains of the Day,* for example, is the torrent of feeling he never allows to surface, the life story of companionship and expression he never allows to rise past his polite restraint. Ishiguro says that in his novel *A Pale View of Hills* he has told a story based on vacuums—holes devoid of information but surrounded by tremendous expectation. The novel begins with a woman making a bold announcement about her daughter's suicide, then saying nothing more about this. Instead, she tells another story. It may be too painful sometimes, Ishiguro says, to tell something directly. So the oblique story carries in other ways what it does not tell.

2. Characters in Edward Hopper's paintings—the café couple in *Nighthawks,* for example, or the woman with the letter in *Hotel Room,* the couple in *Sea Watchers,* the lone figure in *Automat*—are at the end of some story not specified. They sit still, remember-

ing. Some episode of excitement, of coherence has passed, and left them in their silence. (This suggests the exercise of writing what one Hopper character will never tell another, or writing one of your own memories in the voice of a Hopper character, or writing the dialogue of the couple when they first met, or a monologue of inner thoughts by one, then the other.)

3. Goethe said, "The beginning and end of all literary activity is the reproduction of the world that surrounds me by means of the world that is in me." Edward Hopper kept this quotation in his wallet, and told friends, "To me, that applies to painting from memory."

4. H. E. Bates reports that he would regularly write quick biographies of people he glimpsed on trains or in parks in the anonymity of London. He would intuit from the carriage of the body, the set of the face, the helpless expressions of hand and eye a whole life predicament. These sketches became the basis of his fictional characters. On several occasions, he found out by chance the truth of his intuitions—with a glimpse, he had seen it all.

5. Emerson had this to say on the use of familiar things in art: "In every work of genius we recognize our own rejected thoughts; they come back to us with a certain alienated majesty. Great works of art have no more affecting lessons for us than this. They teach us to abide by our spontaneous impressions with good-humored inflexibility, then most when the cry of voices is on the other side."

6. Question: How can writers draw on their reservoir of memory without being limited to strict autobiography? As someone said, how can we avoid "spending our capital" and instead learn to write forever on the *interest* from our capital: fiction based on the library of memory *transformed*? Every vivid memory holds some

essential truth about your vision of the world. How to refract this through characters?

7. Someone said that all you have forgotten becomes compost for the garden of your imagination.

8. One rich beginning for writing of all kinds is the three-thousand-to-ten-thousand-word autobiography recommended by Carol Bly in her book *The Passionate, Accurate Story.* (I do urge a reading of that book with all its richness about this project.) One approach is to write episodes of a page or two in the order they occur to you, without regard to chronology or "importance" of the memory. This becomes a basis for poetry, fiction, essay, and other forms, in addition to strict memoir.

9. This all suggests an exercise for writers, by which we can draw on memory but produce fiction. We can savor strangers around us and invite them to become fictional characters in possession of our own most vivid recollections. I invite everyone to try some variation of the following:

Write your random autobiography of ten thousand words in a series of episodes garnished with maximum detail. No order, no development, just rich moments told in particular. Get five to ten pages into this project this week, and then keep going until you reach ten thousand words.

Collect a set of characters from observation of strangers in life and art: half-page profiles of intuited wants, fears, family backgrounds, adventures, losses, weaknesses, visions, and other internal and external particulars—just start taking dictation on your guessing faculty as you observe characters around you.

Do some listing and clustering in which you graft several of your own memories onto particular characters you have observed (it might be wise to change gender, age, and social situation so you don't end up writing about yourself, or someone very much like yourself).

Write a story in which two or more of these characters meet and tell some truth, and hide some truth. You are becoming the stranger and telling your new hybrid life with full freedom.

The idea is for characters you half-observe and half-invent to remember and enhance things you actually did in ways that make them discover things you have never known.

10. You don't write your whole life, but the vivid parts that have stayed with you. You don't write a character's whole story, but the deft fragments that must be told. The whole secret in writing is the ability to recognize the good line, the part that sings, the sliver that is new, and old, and deeper than what surrounds it—idea, rhythm, insight—the whole work of writing is to hone this habit of selection. We find the small, rich beginning that speaks, and we let it grow according to an imaginative logic of its own. End of sermon.

And then we did some short writing exercises to test these ideas, shared some of our discoveries, and the three hours were over. We had a major project ahead of us, for any who chose to carry out this sequence. And the next week's class was pretty much taken care of, as we would share passages from the autobiography and report what was happening as we married personal memory to fictional character. If I were to arrive then too prepared with new lessons, the unfolding of this one would be crimped in the bud. Make a note to myself to step back next week, and hear some work in progress.

It may be, in fact, that this approach to teaching is the educational equivalent of what Ishiguro was talking about. Maybe the vacuum surrounding the teacher's intention becomes the opportunity for students telling stories to each other—the deepest source of learning.

"How long did it take you to prepare for class?"

"All my life."

READING THE CUTBANK GRIEF

I roam the classics, a forest of treasures,
and love their elegant balance of style and substance.
Inspired, I lay down the book I was reading
and let words pour from my brush.
—Lu Ji, c. 300

How many teachers have told you, "If you want to be a writer, start by being a reader"? I've heard it so often I say it to myself. I'm constantly copying titles of books recommended by friends into the back pages of my pocket notebook. I have a long list of intentions there. Books spill from the shelves at home, and a locked storage unit in town holds what I call my library. But the act of reading, in my writing life now, is a rare indulgence.

My father used to tell about my behavior in childhood when the family visited our local library. Everyone would scatter to browse along the shelves, tasting many books, and return to the entrance with an armload at the time we had agreed to meet. But I was different, he said. I would pull out one book, seemingly at random, and sit on the floor right there to begin reading. An hour later, I was still there, having found nothing but that one book.

Maybe this is why I went to one college for twelve years. Maybe this is why I married the first woman I kissed, and stayed eighteen years. Maybe this is why I sleep in the same hollow of ground below Mount Jefferson every August. Maybe this is why I don't leave Oregon.

The length of my required reading list in graduate school brought me a perverse pride. After getting direction from my faculty advisors, I typed the list with my Olympia portable on a scroll of paper six feet long, rolled and tied it with linen string, and carried it like a prophet. Oh, I was a scholar! I would toss open my scroll with a flourish to find I had checked off O. B. Hardison's *Pagan Rite and Christian Drama,* A. B. Lord's *Singer of Tales,* and Shippey's *Wisdom Literature.* On to E. Talbot Donaldson! I doggedly read every book on the list, and that exercise killed something in me. Now I can hardly read a book to the end. If the book bores me, I put it down in a hurry, and turn my gaze, if I can, to a tree, or a distant bird, and my mind to thoughts of my own. If the book inspires me, often I am stricken with a feeling of mortality by its truth, and ask myself: "If I have time to read this, shouldn't I be writing? Life's not that long." Then I lay down the book, and words pour from my pen.

Should one have to choose? Can't a life be gifted with reading books, as well as writing? That would be my ideal. Maybe when I'm old.

This hinge event, this pivot—closing the book I have been reading and opening my notebook to write—honors an old paradox about reading, for the verb "to read" originally meant both to decipher a text and to explain a mystery. (I know this from my study of all those books.) Discussing the origins of the Old English verb *rǽdon,* "to read," the *Oxford English Dictionary* tells us "The original senses of the Teutonic verb are those of taking or giving counsel, taking care or charge of a thing. . . . The sense of considering or explaining something obscure or mysterious is also common to the various languages, but the application of this to the interpretation of ordinary writing, and to the expression of this in speech, is confined to English and Old Norse." In other words, fair reader, to limit "reading" to deciphering what has already been written is an unusual constriction of the possible.

The original "reader" was a teller, a story maker, a diviner, just as the original "lecturer" was someone who read a text aloud (from Latin *lĕgere,* "to read"). So, in English, the writer is reading, and the reader is teaching. No wonder we can get confused. Without the salutary act of writing as a prevalent habit in school, the isolated act of reading other people's writing may kill the pupil's own voice and pleasure.

The idea of the "reader" divining, explaining, telling something mysterious—this rings true for me. Another part of my childhood, outside the library, taught me how to read a landscape to find secrets. The trick is this: You go to the injured place and study what has been exposed. For arrowheads, you find where the wind has scoured away the earth and left just stones and bones on bedrock. To see the root of things, you find where a great tree has fallen, leaving an open crater in the forest's surface cloth of moss and fern. To see into geology, the cutbank is best, where a river or a road has sliced down through time and left the world's making abundantly revealed. In memoir, you honor your lonesome times. And in a family, you find where grief has pulled away the veil. The fundamental courage of the writer is to go to that place and express what has been hurt into truth.

Emerson advised us never to read a whole book, for there are too many and life is short. We should, he said, sip the best pages we find, and then close the book and move on. He advocated a kind of intellectual hunting and gathering. A deer does not consume the whole prairie, but takes the most tender and nutritious buds the earth offers, knowing by experience which flavors best give life.

A witness who had been there told me this: At the workshop where Amy Tan first brought her manuscript "The Joy Luck Club," her fellow writers broke the hard news to her: "Amy, there is only one passage in the whole manuscript that speaks in your true voice.

You're going to have to revise the whole thing to match that passage." The story is she did so, and the novel thrives.

I learn from this that the act of writing one's truth requires one to read for zero—to sample the draft like a wine taster, and spit out what does not achieve true vintage. So writing is really an act of reading. You read the landscape of your life and find the places where grief, or fear, or sudden surprise has revealed your truth. Then by reading the best of this experience, you write down one way to tell it. Then you read your first draft to find the places where the language is most your own, most in keeping with what your life revealed. There you have it. Revision is fully active reading, a way to carve your true voice from the words your hands have written.

Open Discovery in the Art of Creative Nonfiction

I have learned from a friend about a legal process called "open discovery." This requires the prosecutor and the defense attorney to hide nothing. Each clue one discovers is given to the other. When all clues have been shared, their work in court is to compose the strongest story of what happened.

My friend said his own research on behalf of an Alaskan boy accused of murder had led him beyond story to myth, to ancient Tlingit tellings that defend our kinship with the earth, with that world where woman marries bear, and the people trace their ancestry direct to salmon, eagle, cedar, and frog. After learning these things, he said, the charge of murder loomed larger, the defendant's plight felt deeper, and the ritual in the courtroom seemed very tame and thin.

As a writer, I wondered how a defender, inquiring through open discovery into one night's crisis, might save a life by getting the story right. Or the prosecutor might find a stronger story. And this makes me want to ask: When we sit down to write, with the open discovery of all we have met, how will the true story crawl through our pens into being? For the story arrives by the struggle of writing what we don't quite know.

A life, or a river, has urgency, goes around the rock in its path, and travels on. We translate this river in many ways. In our writing, we might call this translation "creative nonfiction." We might call it "the literature of information." We might call it "the musical arrangement of passionate fact." It will be an intimate negotiation between writer and reader, in the presence of the actual, informed by some mutually discovered thread of understanding. That thread will always be there, for the writer is the kind of teacher who invites others into the room where the evidence can be displayed. The writer lets the process of open discovery unfold.

Maybe it's the same with teaching. Some days when I tell my wife I'm not ready for class, she tells me I should not have more answers than my students have questions. I should be alert to meet them in the presence of their own writing. We will negotiate a learning sequence around a set of experiences we share and a common thread we discover.

For the writer, as well as for the reader, creative nonfiction is the search for the most compelling story, or complex of stories, behind a given screen of information. In the process of the essay, memoir, fact-based sermon, informing prayer, traveler's journal, vivid profile, family saga, or other genre cousin within the tribe of creative nonfiction, the writer and reader share a certain collection of facts, chronologies, physical sensations, places, and a cast of characters. We hold these elements in common, and then we each—like prosecutor and defense attorney—seek the story that makes it all matter.

The story for the writer will be some magnetic wire of meaning that binds the collection of facts into some provisionally satisfying form. Some silk thread will gather the beads. The story for the reader will include the writer's necklace, but will include other possibilities as well, because the facts of the story, the beads, are negotiable currency in the reader's own imaginative economy.

Because the raw material is fact, the writer and reader are partners in the open discovery of meaning. Because the work is literary, the way the facts become story is more important than the facts themselves. We will want to read this story again. And each time we read, new stories may gather into our minds from the same evidence. In all this process, the most enticing experience for me is the discovery of the thread of coherence, the informing idea I don't know until I do. Until this happens, life is random; after this happens, life is mysterious.

You tell me about Alaska winter, in dear detail, with your lit thread of discovery that binds all things—icicle, nose prickle, the sound soft snow makes underfoot, a night dog's bark—and I begin to notice my own thousand and one nights in small-town motels, traveling in the ministry of the word. Or I tell you about traveling in the ministry of the word—and you begin to remember your own travel through mornings and evenings in your family's story. We look at evidence together, and exchange ways of seeing our stories.

Pondering this, I found myself at a conference in Florida, a place I had never been. As I often find in a strange place, I felt like a child newly entering the world. Behind the hotel lay miles of swamp, ribbons of bristling scrub, glittering pools and sloughs and casual streams, and I didn't know the names of anything. I stood in ignorant wonder. That bird flouncing a tail long as a shadow, that stunted tree writhing up from black water, that small frame house trimmed in jade green, with a plaster Madonna in the yard of white sand—I felt them equal to that riverbank in my native Oregon when I was small and amazed, when I told my parents, "I want to go jump in the daylight."

From the hotel, I wandered. The two sailors standing by a woman on the corner, one of them kissing her long and leisurely, while the other smoked a cigarette. The turtle's triangle head pointing up from the black pool a block from city hall. The silk air heavy on my brow. The splayed foot of the lizard on the sidewalk inside my shaggy head shadow. The fine sand of the anthill stirred to frenzy by my fingertip. At dusk, the neon vacancy sign that hurt me. At two A.M., the old man's face on the hotel TV screen without sound. At dawn, the frayed Do Not Disturb tag in my hand.

What is our story? What is mine, and what is yours? My father has died, and my brother. We are about to share a secret you have treasured, and confusions I have treasured. Reading this world, we need each other.

THE RANDOM AUTOBIOGRAPHY

Several years ago I received a manila envelope out of the blue from my aunt Helen:

> Dear Kim:
> I'm sending you this because it seems important to me that one should be known really well by at least one person. And I guess you are it.

What followed was a five-page single-spaced typescript titled "My Life," which began with my aunt's first memory, c. 1906, and then an early recurring dream, then a multitude of childhood sensations and confusions, a series of cryptic signposts along the way, and finally a trio of epiphanies.

When I asked Helen about this project, the next time we met, she claimed she stole the idea from Harry Truman. On a certain wedding anniversary, it seems, Mr. Truman presented his wife with a chronological record of their years together. When Helen showed me the Truman version, however, the entries were decidedly concise. One I remember:

1943   A bad year.

Her own episodes, on the other hand, were often lyrical bursts within a sequence that included events, sensations, judgments:

Living on the high prairie in a little shack.

View from the top of the windmill.

Still summer evenings—barking of a distant dog.

Mother very ill. Going with Daddy to the barn at night to kneel down in the hay and pray that Mother get well. The lantern light, the sweet-smelling hay and the contented horses munching.

Then there were tiny glints of information with huge implication:

Intimations—tough times ahead. "You are different."

And this vein continued in a series of setbacks:

High School—sorrows.

First year of teaching. Hell.

But scattered through her chronicle of tough times, these small reprieves:

A little hidden valley.

The fragrance of mint fields.

Delightful give and take.

On my own—the road to salvation.

When I asked my aunt, at our next tea party, how she came to remember these particular moments from the long sweep of her life, she answered, "When an event, no matter how small, makes a strong impression on my emotions, it remains with me forever." Her power of deep feeling, it seems to me, had been source to both her difficulty and her safety.

She concludes "My Life" by reporting, "Once on the radio I heard

Einstein say that 'Mystery is the most beautiful thing in the Universe.' This remark made a deep impression on my mind." And then a small suite of expanded moments from long life: "Into the depths of mystery I toss these small but crystal-clear memories."

I cherish my aunt, her honesty, the toughness of her tenderness. As her nephew, I am privileged to possess this window into her life, these rich pages. As a writer myself, as a writing teacher, I want to know how this sense of detailed life story can be available to me before I become an elder. Without the advantage of a full long life of pondering, ordering, and wise understanding, how can I find for myself, and invite my students to find, a way to catalog the treasury of life experience for use in writing?

One summer my father came home from a writing workshop with a text written by someone in his group, a text called simply "Autobiography." This text has since transformed my teaching. Composed by a writer named Mary Ann Larson (someday I hope to meet her), this autobiography has a special quality—it *seems* to be completely random, and yet it is not. It dispenses with chronology. It ignores any sense of the importance or nonimportance of particular life episodes. Every memory is welcomed as it arrives. This writer simply lists recollections in a kind of musical sequence as they come to mind. At times one incident might follow another by the bridge of a color, or a time of day, or the sound of a word:

I once screamed at
my boss
in anger,
and have been
falling-down drunk
on Irish Mist.
I once kissed an anarchist.

Other times, the writer had simply done two things twice—and by this they fit together: two losses, two visits to the same town. How does a life make sense, after all? One way a life makes sense for a writer is found by roving through memory without the shackles of orderly time, the screen of merit, or the rigors of rationality. By this model I can invite myself, and my students, to be as hospitable to each memory as a dog welcoming its master home. I welcome the next random recollection, and then the next, and the next, just as Mary Ann Larson does in her conclusion:

> My silver baby cup
> is all banged up.
> I am
> licensed to practice.

When I asked a group of young students in Wyoming to write their own version of the random autobiography, one young woman wrote a random sequence about lost friends, a yellow puppy, working at the discount store, messing up and making it right, and the one great love. When I read that student's piece to a class in Oregon, one young man responded with a poem about watching life through the lens of a needle and crying inside his mother's ashes. And when I read his poem to a group of forest rangers in Washington state, they wrote lists of life events that brought into strangely inevitable sequences a grandfather's arthritic hand offering a dime, a first kiss, boot camp, realizing not all fathers yell, and the feeling of truth leaking through a pen.

In these and many other experiments with this exercise in class, I see how the random autobiography invites each writer to freely shift from particular observation to long assessment, and then back to the particular. The result often becomes a compelling text alone and, at the same time, a table of contents for future writing. Each line in the random list could be a chapter title for a book of essays, a collection of poems, a song list. Episodes talk to each other, and each cries out for fuller treatment. Every ratchet step in this progressive list becomes a subject for expansion in a journal, story, poem, essay, letter, or more deliberate memoir. Sometimes I ask students to use their random autobiography as a series of beginning points for an extended series of writing invitations. "You have written your own syllabus. In how many different directions might these topics now lead you over time?"

Often my workshops begin with a reading of one example or another of a random autobiography, and then the invitation for students to write their own, beginning, again and again, with some variation of "I remember." Every time I lead a group in this exercise I write my own, and every time I write my own I come up with new episodes:

I swung out on the rope and thought I would die, letting go.
This other time, we left the road at fifty, into darkness.
Nothing was safe, but death would surely come, so
     we had to try everything once.
I saw my aunt's true self for the first time
     the moment she died.
The moment our daughter was born, I knew
     she would be a tough one.
I shipped the oars, closed my eyes, and slept.
I carved a girl's name on an alder tree—
     thirty years later we spoke for the first time.
I was in Rock Springs, Wyoming, standing
     by the copy machine in the library when
     someone said, "We're bombing Bagdad . . .
     how many copies are you making?"

I could not marry again until my father died.

   Is that true? It happened.

Boring meetings are times of ripe imagination.

Why are so many of my most precious memories

   the times I did things so frightening

   I swore I would never do them again?

I've tried this exercise with groups of writers perhaps a hundred times, and each time I find new stories, glimpses, moments that have been waiting in my subconscious to be summoned. Sometimes the cluster comes in disturbing ways, and as a writer I rejoice:

   I remember getting caught for shoplifting, for being naked,

      for forgetting where I was supposed to be.

   Sometimes you have to do what you can't justify.

   I remember the old black man who ran into my rental car, and

      called me "Honey."

   I remember the water tower, the church roof, the cemetery fir

      tree, and all those other dangerous places

      I tried in my own way to "get high."

   I remember that book about the women who dove for pearls.

   When I drank from the Menhir Spring, what happened to me?

   Digging a hole in sand to be in.

   That snake in the lawnmower.

   I shot at my brother.

Raw, strange, troubling. Disturbing in a rich, demanding way. What are these things I have silently been carrying? What an odd person I am! How might each glimpse be a seed for a story? I can't deny what made me. Best proclaim it now. I shot at my brother? Yes. He survived me, and later died by his own hand. I guess I have been very efficiently not thinking about that for a while, but now a hint from my writing asks me to tell more.

For a writer, the urge to tell more is one kind of intense happiness. The random autobiography springs this sensation on the class. You might write your random autobiography as a hero, selecting random episodes of triumph. Or your random autobiography as a failure, remembering lapses large and small. Your life as a thinker, as a collector of numbers, as an observer of quiet things, as a lover, a wanderer, a dreamer. I like going back and forth with this exercise between the generalist (like my Aunt Helen, or Mary Ann Larson, quoted above) and the specialist, by focusing on one thread in the weave. From a focused version of the random autobiography, you might select a set of integrated details for subsequent development: "Seven Episodes of Dancing," "Three Losses and One Recovery," "Random Beauties in Winter." The exercise thus provides both the trick of beginning (it's just a random list, after all) and the abundance of resonant episodes intuitively collected.

With the random autobiography, we have much important work to do, for everyone has a multitude of places to begin.

SENTENCE AS RIVER AND AS DRUM

When I left college to conduct an oral history project in the 1970s, I learned how the spoken language is performed in the key of "and." A storyteller ends each "sentence," each episode in the long recollection, with the word "and," which simultaneously holds the floor from interruption and links one action to the next. This makes the music of one's life feel endless.

At the same time I was observing this performance quirk, I was troubled by the way school had taught me to write interminable prosy sentences, with proof piled upon proof in classy rhetorical structures that left me breathless if I tried to read them aloud. I had learned too well. As someone beginning to write—to write the stories I was hearing in the world with the language habits I had learned in school—I felt the need both to unreel and to reign in my utterances. So, when I became a teacher of writing, I began to use the twin exercise of the long and short sentence to make each student's repertoire more pliable. Each mode tempers the other.

The idea is simple. First, I invite an assembly of writers to compose a sentence that goes on for at least a page—and no fair cheating with a semicolon. Just use "and" when you have to, or a dash, or make a list, and keep it going. After your years of being told not to, take pleasure in writing the greatest run-on sentence you can.

After doing this exercise some fifty times myself, I think I've begun to learn the atmospheric opportunity of the sentence that never has to make a hard decision. As always, I comply with my own request, writing without stopping until I come to the lower right corner of my page, and then I put a title on the monster I have created:

A Life of Art in a Busy World

Could my writing be the river that winds through the obstacles of my life, flowing in its own way, without conflict, so sure of its own relation to gravity that it unfurls its long story past clock and meal, past child and loving wife, inquiring gently through dream and waking, flowing undisturbed and undisturbing past the mailbox, curling and eddying softly past the edges of deadline and annual report, suffusing budget and application and prospectus, carrying little rafts of poetry and barges of prose gracefully through the channel deepened by fear and scoured by grief, urging my intention effortlessly through thickets of disbelief, mildly passing no and yes and maybe on its journey to lower and lower ground, moving easily, flooding with clear water and light the lowest reaches I can find, without any destination but down, without any intention but vital motion through, without any agenda but inclusion, buoyancy, permission, carrying the living scent of one place to the hunger of another, flowing nameless and pure, eager, without ambition, disguised as the world itself traveling through the world?

Then we shake out our writing hands, take a blank page, and write from the upper left to the lower right corner again, but this time letting no sentence be longer than four words (but every sentence must have a subject and a verb). Again, I try the exercise along with everyone, and then release my cramp by adding a long and languid title:

The Realm Where Writing Can Happen Even When You Are So Busy You Can't Write Long but You Can Still Write All the Time Because You Have Watched How Rivers Move

Writing takes time. Life takes time. There's your problem. Can they happen together? They can. Rivers have the key. Rivers pass rocks. There is a way. A rock sits heavy. The river goes around. The mountain rises. The river cuts down. Life gets complex. Writing gets simple. There is a crevice. A moment opens. Writing takes possession. Queens rule small countries. Kings preside over jewels. Wives master hard times. Husbands can learn. Writing braids a rope. Each strand is small. Dreams are filaments. Conversations are strong wire. Family stories weave everything. It all connects. Novels forge rivers. Every little thing counts. Do you believe? Do you want this? Others haunt arenas. Your writing inhabits threads. There are ways. Believe. Write. Be patient. Be bold. It will come together. Gather all things. Travel through time. Harvest gold. Be hospitable to everyone. Leave everyone. Enter your cell. Be the lucky prisoner. Your words are rain. Be free as rain. Tell it all. Rivers have ends. So do you. Be big. Let go.

An odd piece, but I'm fond of it, and I find some lucky nuggets: "Be the lucky prisoner." I like that. And more important than the success of either exercise is that I have reminded myself of the true elasticity of the sentence. In the midst of a run of long sentences, sometime soon, I will remember to embed a small one. Life needs contrast. And in the midst of drumbeat assertions, sometime soon, I will remember to let my cello speak an aria.

The exercise of the long sentence may help me discover connections among many things, all gathered into the net with the simple sticky magnetism of "and." The exercise of the short sentences may help me discover the multiplicity of divergent opportunity within a single subject. I enjoy both. Together, they contribute to the preliminary calisthenics of our writing workshop: Which was easy? Which was hard? Why? As we write, let's watch for opportunities to be concise, and then inclusive, breaking the boundaries of the acceptable in order to be a river, and be a drum. Rivers have long rhythms. Drums roll.

On one occasion, I found myself writing a short story in the space of a single long sentence, and then *Harper's* took it. Now I'm spoiled. Why do it any other way?

The Good Son

So I'm climbing toward smoke on the fourth floor, and the boss is still swinging the ladder into place and I'm already climbing as fast as I can, and I'm thinking just like I always do on the way up, "Maybe I'm not cut out for this," but at the same time I'm noticing the skid tape on the rungs is getting worn again, and I'm mad at the boss to let the truck get run down like this, but it's bad to be thinking of anything but my immediate safety when I get that high—third ladder section, and they get narrower as you go up—but I always think of all kinds of things as I climb, I mean it could be my last thoughts, so why not make them good, and at the same time I'm curious what I'll see over the top, like is it going to be someone dead, or passed out smoking in bed, or (like this one time) these two making love behind closed doors while the kitchen burns, so you get ready for anything, and about then I notice the balcony I'm aimed for has the rusted railing about to fall off, which is true half the time, and the smoke coming out the window looks yellow, could be toxic, but I also notice this girl on the balcony to the side, leaning on her railing watching me, and she's a good looker, and first I notice she's calm, so that sets me at ease, because my heart still races when I get near the top, and then through the grating I notice how short her dress is, and I mean I'm not trying to see it or anything, but I am coming up from below and it might be my last time, and the boys always say a girl, the good you feel for her is the eleventh commandment, the heart of life, what you praise and honor, because I could be dead in two minutes if it's bad, and if the boys going up the stair can't break through the door once I tell them to, some kind of explosion, some flare-up, and so the girl smiles and I smile, I obey with all I've got, not wanting anything but that moment, and there's this sweet religion between us, a whole testament braided in the air just the length of one breath, but then I'm climbing like mad again, climbing past her, watching my fingers grab the rungs, and then I'm over the railing and low in the room and guess what, the smoke is only six inches down from the ceiling, and there's grandma on the couch sleeping, and the neighbors banging on the door, and I follow the smoke into the kitchen and it's nothing but cabbage cinders in a pot on the stove, so I'm on the radio to the boss with two words, "burnt cabbage," and he shoots back, "what?" and I say, "everything's cool," and I'm over and out, but I can't stop thinking of the grandma, is she okay, and the girl, will she still be there, and so I kill the gas at the stove, and knock the pan into the sink and smother the burnt cinders of cabbage, and then I'm padding out to the living room to wake her, and she's already smiling, she's having a dream through all this, and I see in the smoky light her face is beautiful when she smiles, and she must have known some good times, and I can hardly bear to touch her, to wake her, but she needs some air, so I put my hand on her shoulder and she opens her eyes, looks up at me and says— "Again?"—but she can't understand a thing I say, and I know she must be deaf, so she didn't hear the neighbors pounding or our siren, and I help her to the window for some air, and then it comes to me we have been here before, only Pierre climbed last time, and when he found the burnt cabbage he was so disgusted he wouldn't say a another thing about it, and I see grandma is fine, the way she coughs and smiles and looks down as embarrassed as a girl, but not exactly embarrassed, maybe more like in heaven to have a visitor and all this attention, but I have to take my leave, not touching the rail, but onto the ladder, and I turn around and there's the girl, just below me, and I'm climbing down past her, and as I go by so close I could touch her she asks me if Madame is okay, and I say yes, and then somebody starts honking—of course on this narrow street we have traffic backed up everywhere, and the boss doesn't need the radio with me in view, he's shouting for me to get down off the ladder if the situation is under control, and I look at the girl and she's enjoying all the shouting as much as Madame enjoys the attention, and she's enjoying me, too, and I know exactly how slow I can go down the ladder to keep the boss under control—one rung, two—and the old woman is waving from her window, and the girl is waving from the balcony, and the wind blows her dress and her hair and there's just a little cabbage smoke, but it's almost gone, and there's just a wisp of perfume, and the girl's smile is wide open, and I obeyed, feeling it when she smiled, so I live, and the old lady is so happy I came to visit, and I'm going down slow—all that honking and shouting on the street, and I'm thinking, like I always do on the way down—I didn't die, I didn't even die.

WRITING IN THE OPEN

Where does your writing actually get done—in time, and in space? What have been the conditions that, perhaps unpredictably, produced your most interesting work? Are there places or times you would consider impossible to write? Are there places or times you believe would assure you happy writing?

I remember thrifty undergraduate days, when I wrote most of my poems in a closet and on the backs of envelopes. I stacked my clothes on the bedroom floor and politely departed from my roommate by retiring to the closet, where I had a desk and chair and lamp. I was thinner then, could fold myself compact. (In a dream once, I had a narrow desk on which to write poetry—so narrow that only short lines were possible.) Sometimes I miss that closet. With the light on and the door closed, there was incredible focus to the page before me.

A friend asked his class if there were conditions that would make writing impossible. They were full of ideas. In fact, most of them described the conditions of their lives, and tried to convince him that these conditions made writing impossible: work, family, telephones, housework, errands, fatigue—all the building blocks of daily life. Faced with this, my friend rashly vowed to write a story in the hour before his own wedding. He did it. But then he couldn't find anyone who wanted to hear his new story—we were all *very* busy.

The fact is, the act of writing itself is the only possible time and place. The immediate vertigo of the moving pen, of a rattling keyboard, of spontaneous utterance while walking is where the muse resides. You write where there is an opening. But how to begin?

I don't begin, the writing does. I don't try, I yield. I have written in trees, on planes, by flashlight, during symphonies, by the light of a movie screen, while driving (I've lately sworn off this), during faculty meetings, and while making dinner. Every shirt must have a pocket, and every pocket a notebook and a pen. Once the muse bites, it's delicious anywhere. For the act of writing begins before you consciously know if you have time. Your hands do it.

What is so right about a good coffee shop, for example? What so sets the tone of creative endeavor that the whole room seems to partake of the buzz? I think immediately of a Paris café, where when you look up from your own writing, half the people around you are writing as well, scribbling away with fountain pens at their letters and diaries and nicely bound notebooks. I love the slogan of a Parisian pen maker: *A chaque style, un stylo,* "for every style, a pen"—as if the pen itself made such a difference. But perhaps it does. A Parisian friend inquires, "What is your favorite nib—not the pen, but the nib, the working tip?" She favors twenty-four-carat gold, fine, and gives me the name of the maker. With the right pen, in the right café, the hum of some talk provides a quality of intimate seclusion that is difficult to match when alone. I have a favorite café—and in winter I take the table by the heater. And I have a favorite table in a favorite library in Paris, and a favorite grate where the homeless gather to curl in the cold, and a favorite threadbare apartment where the toilet is a hole in the closet floor. Writers are at home in a homeless place, if stories throng there. Shakespeare and Company Bookstore in Paris: If you will work an hour a day, or read a book a day, you can stay for free. The tone is just right. The night the thief smashed the glass and broke in there, we residents ended the incident by discussing pens with a pair of gendarmes under the streetlight: *"Mais oui, le Waterman. . . ."*

The college where I work, for all its efficient buildings in lovely settings, does not possess a room suitable for writing a poem. There is a writing center, of course, which is helpful, and a writing lab filled with computers. There is a lounge in the English Department, and there are classrooms and study rooms and a fine library with tasteful lamps on solid tables. But none of this is quite right for writing a poem. Why?

Well, a college is a strangely industrious place. Monkish cells for solitude, on the other hand, and locations for the devotion of spiritual work, retreats for true creation, tend to be compromised by telephones, the bustle of hearty colleagues, and the slow starvation of the lecturer. It is strangely debilitating to be surrounded by people who know, experts. Maybe I can sneak away to a biology laboratory, when it is empty, or that one corner desk in the law school library with a forest view. But at this school, just about the only place conducive to creation on a regular basis is the lucky trance of in-class writing, when the group is eager, and we go into the river of stories together.

Am I being precious about this? Doesn't true desire find a way, anywhere? I write these words at the table a hundred miles from home where I sat, in retreat three years ago, when the phone rang to tell me my father had died. The next time I sat at this table, the phone rang to tell me my beloved aunt had suffered a stroke. On both occasions, I arose immediately and departed from my writing for some months. I return here, hopeful, and I write as fast as I can.

We are on a tough road in good company, we writers. When we gather in a place, when we read each other's words, we can be touched by a kind of truth serum, which is infectious, and makes us want to tell everything, disregarding all safety and convenience. It will be right to do so, for none of us is immune. We share our secrets eagerly, like the sick embracing each other, while others in the world around us pull away into what they seem to believe are such wholesome silences.

Lead me to the telling place.

PEPPER

In college I signed up for the class called "Camp Cookery" just because I was curious and had Wednesday nights free. It turned out to be a required course for all geology majors, and we twelve men rolled up our sleeves, put on our aprons, and were instructed by Miss Pelch in the mysteries of mock apple pie and the secrets of the stove.

Imagine a row of eleven pies baked golden brown, and then my cinder.

One night Miss Pelch told us a private trick, which I have never used in cooking, but which has saved my writing often from lapsing to the simply sweet: pepper in the apple pie.

"The tongue is fooled," she said, "if you sneak a pinch of pepper along with the cinnamon and sugar. Fooled to a deeper bliss."

Is that true in cookery? I know it's true in writing. Pepper in the prose, pepper in the poem can make the sweetly sentimental return to life and vigor. I guess we could call this edge, or contrast, but I prefer to think of it as pepper. It is that secret ingredient in the arts that intensifies the sense of the particularly beautiful in the real. The photographer Joel Meyerowitz, in his portraits, seeks what he calls "life's jewelry" on the body: freckles, birthmarks, scars. These, with the light of spirit in the eyes and the grace of tired slouch or dancer's balance, authenticate the beautiful. As my sculptor friend says of her injured nudes in Carara marble, "My work is beautiful, but it is not pretty."

My own reminder of this trick resides in the following set of notes

I made when visiting the parents of a writer friend up near Battle Ground. The visit was a sweet one in many ways—the wild rabbit haunting the garden, the cherries spilling crimson along the branches of their fertile tree, the rose bush seeming to prop up the old barn, and in the kitchen, canaries singing in their cage. But all this was made more powerful by the hard things that worked against easy pleasures, and deepened their flavor:

1. Mr. Caldwell, old Irish, is sitting in his chair sucking on a cigarette at eighty-seven. He wears the suspenders and the powerful body of a working man, a hero. He does not recognize his own son:

    "Hey, old man, do you know me?"

    "You *look* familiar."

    "I'm Keith!"

    "Do you know the best trade?"

    "I'm your *son!*"

    "*Of all the trades a going, your begging is the best, / For when a man is tired, he can lay down and rest.*"

    "Mom, he doesn't know me."

    "He knows you're familiar. He *likes* you."

    "Dad, tell my friend a story—about your logging days."

    "Well . . . it was always easier to carry a dead man out of the woods, but when they were still alive, you had to be careful how you held 'em."

2. Outside, at the pasture's edge, an old oak straddles the sunlight, magisterial.

    "There's the oak where my great-great-grandmother dropped dead of a heart attack carrying a pail of water to the workers in the field."

3. In the hymn silence of the barn, on a shelf over the threshing floor, a sheaf of wheat lies bundled where it was cut by horse-drawn combine fifty years ago. Beside it, the old man has nailed to the hand-hewn beam a withered possum's foot.

4. "Yeah, Mom loves her canaries. She kept breeding them, until she got about three hundred, and then it was odd for a while."

5. In the late afternoon sun, the cows are moving slowly toward the barn.

   "You know, there are three kinds of dairies: Grade A, Grade B, and Grade C. They never made much ice cream out of *our* milk."

6. The family cemetery is a calm refuge, drowsy with shade.

   "He told us to plant potatoes on his grave, so whenever he got hungry he could reach up and pick one. He also told us to pour whiskey on his grave now and then. We said, 'Sure, we'll pour whiskey on your grave, but we're going to drink it first.'"

WHY WRITE?

The answer must be pleasure. If I don't write for pleasure, I want to adjust the conditions until I do. The pleasure of immersing myself in stories wakes me in the morning, and makes me reluctant to retire at night. So much of life is attrition, and how precious the realm of creation, seeing stories and poems come into existence, as if from nowhere, a garden in the open land. As my daughter said when she was young, "I love the way you can impossible make things up on the piano." Me too, with only a pen and a blank scrap. A weaver told me once:

> I'm a good weaver because I love all the steps. I love picking dirt out of a raw fleece, inhaling that rank lanolin. And I love the carding and then the spinning, the controlled slip of a thread turning through my fingers. I love the smell of the dye pot, and the handling of damp hanks of yarn as I pick out the shreds of onion skin and alder bark. I love threading the loom! Lots of weavers hate that part, just wanting to get to the weaving, but I love it—getting the tension right as you roll the warp onto the loom, and threading every end strand through the heddles and the reed. And then the weaving, well, that's pretty great. And then you cut it off the loom, and work it in the water to full it, get it to cohere as a fabric. The only part I don't like is letting it go—sales.

And with writing? I love all the stages—the gathering of shreds from everywhere, notes, letters, reading, sensation, conversation, dreams, and the plain magic of imagination. I love the tools—papers of different tooth and texture, inks, nibs, the cedar of pencil shavings, my computer in its little black bag. A friend insisted I try writing with a good fountain pen on stiff bond on a cool slab of polished marble—on a hot day, with good light. He was right: what a symphony. And I love the jazz of not knowing—yet—where a piece of writing wants to go, and then the taking hold! I love the second genius, when revision takes on the salty vitality of first writing, all over again. And then I love the nit-picking of editing, spelling, sentence detail, and getting the headers to work on my old computer. And I even love scouting for a good home for my child, once the story or essay has grown and needs to set out into the big world. I send her off with gusto: Go, and may the world hear thee.

I remember a student, Karen, who could not speak, but could point with a wand to the letters on the alphabet board taped to the arms of her wheelchair. At home, she could type at quite an amazing speed with her nose. She found such pleasure in making known the secrets within her, we all were humbled. One of her poems, addressed to a friend, seemed to speak for her love of writing itself: "When I see you, I lose the urge to be responsible!" Marvelous Karen.

When the time is right, I like to give an audience or class what I call my quiz—about the human condition. The story goes like this: Once, in the last century, missionaries went to an island off the south California coast and took away all the people there, took them to the mainland to watch over them. Do you know this story? Scott O'Dell wrote the novel *The Island of the Blue Dolphins* imagining how it was for the one who was left behind, the girl who lived on San Nicholas Island for eighteen years alone. In those years, she would long for human contact, but when a ship came, she was suddenly afraid, and would hide. And she could hide very well, for she knew her island with great intimacy.

Finally, the story goes, a group of sailors decided to capture her—to save her, as they called it. They moored their ship, and starting at one end of the island, they marched in a row stretching across the whole island, never out of sight of each other, at a slow walk to the other end. But the woman hid herself away in a crevice, and they missed her. After their line had passed, she came out of hiding, and crouched on a low ridge, watching them all stride north.

But one man had dropped back from the others, and ahead he saw this woman crouched down, humming softly to herself, rocking back and forth as she watched his fellows march away. Silently, he came up to her from behind. He touched her shoulder.

Here is the quiz about our kind: What did she do? Did she leap up to embrace him? Did she run? Did she lose all ability to act—in that frenzy we can feel when life is suddenly too big?

She motioned for him to sit on the earth, and she prepared a meal for him.

The meal may have been a strange one—perhaps some kind of seal meat and roots—but her impulse was the core of all we do, to put before another the pleasure we can, we who are alive at the same time.

It is said then she boarded their boat, and when a storm came up in the crossing, she stood at the prow and sang a song in her own language, and the winds grew calm. She sang in a language known by no one else on earth, for her people by then were gone. And it is said she died soon after. The food they gave her on the mainland was too rich. Hers was the simpler gift. That's how they tell the story.

Why write? Before my time is through, I have a few words I want to put before you, now that you have touched my shoulder, coming out of nowhere. I want them to be the best I have, to squander everything. We might never meet again.

ROSIE'S BOOK OF SAYINGS

A standard question in literary life is "What book most influenced you on your path to becoming a writer?" Many answers are possible, and the wonderful thing is that any book might be the most important at the moment you are reading. But overall, I realize I have an odd answer: The most important book for me was the first one I wrote—or helped write. My parents called it *Lost Words,* and it was a compendium of the unusual things the four children in my family said when we were small. Both our parents were teachers, especially alert to what we said. In his own daily writing my father wrote down his favorites.

This book is important not because it is unusually brilliant. Every child I have met has unique insights and ways of expressing them. But *Lost Words* was our book. The ideas between its covers were our own philosophic landscape, and the language was our collective creation. My brother, Bret, my sisters, Kit and Barbara, and I together challenged each other to figure out the world, sentence by sentence and question by question. Just because our father was the famous poet in the family did not mean we weren't all thinkers, writers, makers of culture. In *Lost Words* democratic inclusion started in the family and became my career.

I cherish this record, and my own habit of writing down the daily wonders of conversation may have its source in this custom from home.

Kit looking at modern art: "These are just *sort of* pictures, aren't they?"

We bought a car last Monday. Yesterday Barbara was out beside it, tying it with a string—"So the wind won't blow it away."

Today, signing Kim's report card, I suggested writing "Incapable of doing any better." He rejoined that I should say, "Capable of doing much worse."

Remembering his friend after we moved away, Bret looked up at the sky and said, "Does our sky hook onto Donna's sky?"

Our mistakes with the language were so odd that our parents, ethnographers of our exotic tribe, simply wrote down our culture, our art, our errors and discoveries.

When my own daughter arrived, I took up this habit. Little Rosemary, like all kids, had outrageous ways of seeing the world, and of finding ways the language could be bent to serve her needs. She had a penchant for questions that summed up lifetimes in one glint of longing:

Papa, why the music is over?

Can we just go fishing this time all our life now?

She also had a way of taking command with a sweeping claim:

I don't like bad times, Papa, I like our times.

I saw the bash men. They push you down and don't give a hug.

And sometimes she looked at exactly one thing:

The bumblebee is having a drink of water in the blue flower.

Me and Lisa are sitting on the porch watching the beetles go round and round.

I peeked and I peeked and I found a raisin in my cereal.

Sometimes she simply described her own actions, delving for understanding:

It's time for me to lie down and cry!

"Turn!" said a voice, and she turned.

When I was dancing, my feet were talking about the music.

And then there were times when her mind went off like a fire that could not be stopped:

[charging around the corner of the house at dusk] Dad! I came to Earth on a rocket, and *you* walked. Look! There are blueberries on this Earth. And look, a house! Let's go in it and see if there's a bed for me. There is! And a blankie! Look outside—raspberries! I love this Earth. It's the only one with magic. I sprinkled magic on the air and it made this Earth magic! All this stuff is new! The other Earth by Japan and Disneyland doesn't have magic. Would you like some? Here, put it in your pocket so it won't fly away. I love this one Earth. Can we live here forever?

Dad, when you sang "Clementine" my heart gave a big beat and hurt me. When my heart hears the song my heart really loves it, and so it gives a big beat because it can't talk to say it really wants to hear it again over my lifetime. I don't want to be mean for you and for us. All the people in the world have to have a chance to love and to be careful. You only have one side to be happy. Surprised is great, but scared is not. That's all. The end. You have to try!

Old Gramcracker played his cello, and he died about six months ago, but before he even died he made my hands and feet, and he is buried way up in the snowy mountains and no one can see where he is buried—up where there are twenty-two rivers and twenty-two mountains and twenty-two fires and twenty-two rocks all in a ring around where he is buried. But only the tiny birds can fly there in the morning in a summer day. His mom was an old friend of mine, too. He calls me his Gram. Dear old Gramcracker, at night he howls like an owl. I wish we could go this night to where he is buried, but we can't because there are slick mountains, and tall fires, and a river that goes a thousand miles long. Listen! "Howl!" That's Gramcracker.

My child reminds me of my childhood, and my childhood reminds me of infinite possibility, and also the beauty of limitation, the exact treasure of now:

But Dad, girls named Rosemary don't die. I'm going to be true!

You know that person bigger than everyone whose name is God? I'm hungrier than God.

The skunks blow their horns and make suddenly smoke!

More recently, our son, Guthrie, has taken over the role of the source for such expressions. At three he pointed out to us his principle for how life works:

You get what you don't want, and then the spirit of what you do want comes to you.

Or he points to a fashionably dressed woman:

Look at that lady dressed in tarantula fur!

Or he wants to help everyone:

> If there were monsters in this world who never said "please," we would never know what they wanted.

And life stretches before him:

> When I grow up, maybe I'll marry a deer. I could ride on his back. I wouldn't need to ride in cars or trains.

And sometimes he turns philosopher:

> I wish there could be nothing so we could have another life—no world, no space. Nothing. We could crack open nothing and be birds. Not people. We could fly.

My childhood and my children together teach me to pluck my notebook from my pocket whenever I hear language invented by those around me. For the language is old, yet strangely young. As writers, we are not called upon to be smart, but to be alert to this youth of the possible. The language is our child, our elder, our great treasure, and the writer is the one who simply takes up the lost words of daily life and gives them a book in which to dwell.

SELFISH PLEASURES IN A LIFE OF ART

A Speech to the Graduating Class

What is the speed of life? I remember two sensations from my youth. One, that I would last forever, a euphoria of eternity with the earth. Second, that I would suddenly end, that my whole long life would collapse into a moment and be done, that I would suddenly wake, ancient and finished.

In school, they taught me the speed of light, how a river of sunlight hurtles toward our green earth. They taught me the speed of sound, how an echo, the wail of a departing train sings at a certain speed.

But what about the speed of knowing, the speed of life? I have had to learn these on my own.

A friend once told me, "Kim, on your deathbed you will be unlikely to cry out, 'I should have spent more time at the office!' But you will also be unlikely to shout, 'I should have been Mother Teresa! I should have been Martin Luther King!' The crisis you will be likely to feel, if you don't live right, will be this: 'I should have been Kim Stafford—the one person I had a chance to be!'"

I am trying to do the work, the unusual, eccentric, and crucial work of Kim Stafford.

There is a story in my family that my grandmother's physician, during her pregnancy, prescribed an hour of beauty a day. There is no report of dietary restrictions, exercises. No, she was simply to take her music, or her sunset, or the unworked colors of the quilt spread by the lamp before her. While others did chores, she sat on the porch and watched the slow inevitability of the twilight, heard the crickets chanting the beginning of the world night by night. She was to take the roll of pasture by evening's mist, the looming shape of barn and of elm, the warm September moon hung low over the corn rows. She was to take these things to nourish her child, my mother, within her.

I feast on this story. It teaches me the fundamental practicality of close witness of the world, which is the beginning of art.

What is it like to live your life story, to feed on the beauty meant for you alone, to insist on the conditions that make it possible to live the precise, full life you are here to accomplish? There is a story my brother told me. He stood on a bluff upriver with a group of county planners, looking down at an island in the Columbia, discussing the fate of this morsel of county land. One suggested opening the island for a housing development. Another suggested a marina, another a rock quarry. It was evening. The river glittered in a silver perimeter around the island below them.

"It's beautiful," my brother said.

"You can't eat beauty, Bret," said one of the company. "You can't eat beauty."

I will always believe my brother died by his own hand at the age of forty because he did not eat enough of sunset and wheeling flock of birds and fern that spirals from itself into the most intense green we can stand. He did not feast sufficiently on the mountain at first light, the time when nothing makes sense but the world as it is, directly there before you. He did not act the art of anger, lullaby, blessing, the articulate curse against cruelty that can begin a healing. He was silent about these things, and silence finally took him into itself, drank him up, and he lay still, and was gone.

My mother was born, and my brother died, at this boundary. Cross it, I say to you. Don't wait for the right time. Don't hesitate. Cross into your beauty now. Carry your seeing, your feasting, your selfish pleasures in the art you choose to the place you need to be, and enact what you have to do there. If you are awake, you have no choice.

Life begins with your witness there.

You have been in school, and now you enter the world. You have been rehearsing *Romeo and Juliet,* and as you go forth you will be called to perform *Waiting for Godot.* Whitman tells us that every success will call for the need for a greater effort. You have had school time, and now you will have to invent your time in the midst of working life. What are the odds for you?

I want to answer that question with another: What is the earliest tributary of life experience you can remember that led you to this moment? What filament of childhood fascination began your journey to this day, this graduation, this ending of schooling and new beginning of a life in the way you will choose? Was it a shout of color to your child face, a deep pleasure in the fingers that pinched paint? Was it your cool blue satisfaction in the work of shadows cast down on pavement, or the mesmerizing hum of a story told well? A music in numbers, in creatures, in people bold with a culture all their own? Was it some irrepressible liveliness in the alphabet your fat pencil began to make, a life in the letterforms themselves on your tablet with its pale dotted lines?

Slowly, by turning from what we learn with others to what we learn alone, we begin to have a sense of the speed of our learning, the first few chapters of our own eccentric life story. Where do we practice it? Where may our story happen best? When we leave the lively hive of this school, what larger hive do we seek?

Some years ago, Robert Bly held a company of disciples at bay in my city of Portland, Oregon, as he declaimed to them the life views of that renegade from the Enlightenment, William Blake. Bly was telling us how Blake saw a succession of levels of experience that we might aspire to climb. At the bottom, the very pit for Blake was that dark, low place where we are angry, we are alone, and we are silent. We have all been there. That dark place, in fact, is ultimately a tributary of joy. But it is dark, and seems final at the time. Next above, according to Bly's Blake, is that place where you are angry, you are alone, but you are shouting. The din is terrible, but at least you are expressing what is, for you, your life. It's a step up.

Next above that is that place where we shout—but we shout at each other. We shout truth and lies and injuries and insights in a welter of noise. Next above, we debate in anger, awaiting our turn to deliver vituperative speeches designed to wound, to defeat. Next above that, we may question one another, live by curiosity, begin to give and to welcome gifts of insight. And then it is, said Bly, only a few steps to Blake's "Garden of Lovers," that place of pure union where we identify and join with another in ecstatic harmony.

"And then," said Bly to us, "what is next? What is above this place of bliss?"

A pause. We thought we had reached the peak.

"No ego?" said one participant.

"No!" shouted Bly. "Blake didn't think we had too much ego— we don't have *enough*. We each should be insisting, '*This* is my vision. *See* it!'"

"Mindlessness?" said another.

"No, not mindlessness! A full mind and close attention are only the beginning of the full life Blake wanted for us."

Finally we said, "We don't know, Robert. What is better than the garden of lovers?"

"Next above, and the highest state," said Bly, "is what Blake called 'The City of Art.' This is the state of constant creativity interactive with others."

The City of Art. This hive of making, of human creative frenzy equivalent to nature at its busiest. Can we be a meadow rife with blossoming and bees? Bly says, "The more you interact with others in the making of art, the greater your originality of voice." And I remember the *Tao Te Ching* says, "The more you give to others, the greater your abundance." And Pablo Neruda says, "I would do for you what spring does for the cherry trees."

And I say, "Practice your life story in an art that is your own." What is the best you can do with the best you have? The answer, now, will not come from your teachers. The answer will not come from me. The answer will come from your pain, trying to find out. Your path to your art is your art. You will make of your path a beauty and a puzzling maze.

The answer will come from your dreams, from cruelties by others that call forth generosities from you. The answer will come daily, in small acts of seeing that are tributary to greater acts of making that are tributary to yet greater acts of collaboration with brush and portfolio and gallery and dollar bill and shout and impulse and kiss and new paint and a night that distills sorrow to color and joy to shape and the whirl of all your questions into a few bold strokes.

FAME

I began to lose my innocence about ravishing fame one day when I came to work, sifted the mail on my desk, and opened a letter on New Mexico motel stationery:

> Kim:
>
> I was playing a charity gig down in Albuquerque when I came across one of your songs. It's good. Damn good. I want it. If you have any more that good, I want them too.
>
> —Johnny Cash

With letter in hand, I returned to the outer office and asked the secretary, "*Which* of my friends faked this? Do you recognize the handwriting?"

Mary took the letter from me, and with one glance she went wild.

"That's *his* signature! That's Johnny! I have all his records, and some of them have his writing on them. That's it! That's him!"

What happened next began to instruct me. I bit hard. At last, the big time. At last, my years of slavery to the forlorn cause of unknown literature were about to end. Click, click, click—it all fell into place. Ten years before, I had mailed the lyrics to my "Juliaetta Coffee Blues" to Johnny. He hadn't responded then, but now something had reminded him. My genius had bloomed in his attention. But how did he run across my song—in Albuquerque? It didn't matter. He had it. He could hear my song with big music behind it:

I put a pack of sugar in my pocket for the road—
Better take two, if only I'd knowed
What a woman can do to a man when he's all alone.

Behind my reverie, Mary was still talking.

"He's playing in Portland tonight, you know—him and the . . . what do they call them? 'The Highwaymen': Johnny Cash, Willie Nelson, Waylon Jennings, and Kristofferson—Kris Kristofferson. They're at the coliseum. I wonder if they're all sold out."

In two minutes, I knew they were not, for I was on the phone with plastic in hand, breathlessly reading my credit card number to an operator at Fastix, and then the proud owner of a twenty-dollar ticket to the tall back balcony. I was on my way!

My next move was to check the envelope: sure enough, a Nashville return address. I called my agent in New York.

"Lizzie, Kim. Hey, Johnny Cash wants my song. Should I just send it? Send him the lyrics and score . . . a tape?"

There was a pause on the line, and then Lizzie caught the fever. At last her client of sleepy essays and tasteful poems had broken through.

"Maybe you'd better write him first," she said, "and ask for the best procedure. It may be that I should work with his agent. We better buy some time here. I don't have any experience with country music, but it's probably handled agent to agent." Another pause. "I *could* make the contact, but since he wrote you, it's probably best for you to respond—at first. Good luck, and keep me posted! Okay?"

What should I do until 8 P.M.? College work? Budgets? Course proposals? Shouldn't I head home and start rehearsing for my demo tape? That would be needed soon. Did I know anyone who could really play the guitar? Or should I leave that to Johnny and his people?

From the top row of bleachers, the distant stage was electric blue, and the Highwaymen, those four males at their microphones had strut and cadence down! Song after song in tight rhythm and rich harmonic filled the haze of the auditorium. And after their opening set, the other three stepped back, and Johnny came out alone. His solo began as a kind of talking blues: Down in some little old Southern town . . . a tattered flag on the courthouse pole . . . an old guy on a bench in the park . . . and the narrator—Johnny, my Johnny—asking wasn't that town ashamed to have such a tattered flag? And then, in Johnny's amazing voice, the old man giving it back, no holds barred: Why son, that flag unfurled at Trenton, when the British troops were caught . . . and they shot her through at New Orleans, in the War of 1812 . . . and aboard old Ironsides, she took a shred of holes . . . in the trenches of France . . . Hitler . . . Iwo Jima . . . Korea . . . Vietnam."

Man oh man, he had one big voice, I thought, but his material could use some work. He needed—me. And together . . .

Then I was in the parking lot with the crowd of fans surrounding Johnny's private coach. When he emerged from the coliseum stage door, the dark center in his moving knot of handlers pushing toward the bus, my heart leaped. But I wasn't like the screaming fans surrounding me with stomps and whistles. I'd hold my peace. I wouldn't trouble him tonight. No, I'd write him in Nashville, when he was home and rested. We'd work it all out like professionals.

Helpers pried open the bus door, and as Johnny stepped inside, half a dozen cassette tapes, flung by hopeful songwriters in the crowd, sailed through the slit of the door closing behind him, or clattered onto the pavement.

On reflection, I wasn't sure which song Johnny might have seen. I have friends in the Southwest, but none in Albuquerque. Was it "Juliaetta Coffee Blues" from ten years back? Or could it be the sad one about the old horses, "I Remember the Ride," which I sang in Elko, Nevada, at one of the Cowboy Poetry gatherings?

> I remember the ride.
> There is no Beauty tonight—
> Star is holy and gone to the sky,
> But I remember the ride.

Could it be the "Pocatello" song I had sent around to a few friends, not knowing what else to do?

> Late one night in Walltown, the boys were playin' cards,
> Sippin' at their whiskey, smokin' their cigars—
> Says a cowboy, "Boys, I'm out of chuck! I'd best throw in my hand.
> I've lost my horse, and lost my hat, I've lost the means to stand in
>   Pocatello, Pocatello town."

Or could he be wanting my lament called "Carbon Canyon," which I sang at a friend's wedding in Cheyenne? Did someone record that session? Who knows, I thought. Good work travels in its own way. Come to think of it, Michael Martin Murphey was at that Cheyenne wedding, too, and Ian Tyson.

I wrote Mr. Cash a careful letter, thanking him for his interest in my work and asking the best way to proceed. I remember worrying over which stamp to use to hasten this key document to Nashville— should it be the American flag stamp, or my own favorite at the time, the rose?

I sent the letter, and stood by. I told a few select friends about my vigil. They kindly shared in my excitement. And in about two weeks, a call came from far away—an old friend from clear back in grade school.

"Ah, Kim, I heard by the grapevine that you bought that letter. I'm *really* sorry. We were just talking about you at a party, and had this idea . . . we never thought you'd fall for it . . . sorry sorry sorry."

I was pleasant on the phone, as I remember. "It's nothing." After I hung up, for a moment, fury surged through me. Then sorrow. I felt lost. And then I sat up straight with a new understanding of what I really wanted. I didn't want fame for me. I wanted fame for what I cherish. I wanted the vagabond humor of coffee at that little Juliaetta café to be known. I wanted those old horses in "I Remember the Ride" to be understood by my people, not just me. I wanted Pocatello, that off-beat Idaho city that treated me to story after story with the generosity of the earth itself—I wanted the town we called Poky to receive the affection of strangers, widely and in easy ways, by something I had made. Maybe I wanted my gift to travel, on its own, without my name at all. Let the songs be anonymous, so they be heard. I wanted "Carbon Canyon" on the radio, reaching down from the sky toward the kind of lonely place where it began:

I name you starlight that falls on the hill,
I name you coyote's call, you waver and you trill,
I name you water that slides by a stone
When you set out on your own.

My friends at their party had not known how deeply I wanted this: the voices of the world that had traveled through me now to travel beyond me. That hurt taught me: Johnny Cash won't sing my songs. I must.

Learning from Strangers

Where there is no vision, the people perish.
—Proverbs 29:18, as quoted by JFK,
   November 1963

A friend calls this life "a bridge from before to after." On this bridge, crossing as a writer, a teacher, and a seeker, what shall I do—especially now? I have stories to tell, and ways to begin. But what is my particular calling in the world? My father said vocation means "your job is to find what the world is trying to be." What are we writers trying to be, in these times, and what is our work on behalf of the healing of the world?

When I turned from the TV images the morning of September 11, 2001, to call my mother, she told me, "I'm watching the news. Everyone's saying this is like Pearl Harbor, but I feel it's really our Hiroshima. Now we're part of the suffering of the world."

I remembered my father's account of a strange day in August 1945. A pacifist, an exile from the war-fever in his own country, he was in San Francisco with a group of conscientious objectors on leave from their work camp in the mountains. Sirens went off, cars began honking, and everyone rushed into the streets shouting, "The war's over! A great big bomb! The Japs are finished!"

Surrounded by people consumed by relief and joy, my father and his friends were stunned. "What does this mean?" they asked each other. "How many Japanese people have died? How can this country celebrate their deaths? Where do we go from here?"

Now we know. We went toward the Cold War . . . Korean War . . . War in Vietnam . . . Gulf War . . . and we went toward now. When the twin towers fell, it became our turn to suffer terror against civilians on our soil, and to be stunned by certain Palestinians caught on film shouting their joy.

It was a crucial moment in our history as a nation. By choosing one word over another—calling the event "an act of war" instead of "a crime"—we changed everything. With a word, the power of our nation turned from one path of the possible to another. We declared war on an unknown enemy, then announced we would not distinguish between that enemy and anyone we considered friendly to that enemy, and then we struck back. The Crusades again.

I waited for the newscasters to ask, "How did compassion die in the hearts of those desperate men? What killed their wish to live? If we are truly powerful, how can we change the conditions at home and abroad that brought this terror?" The answer, I believe, is that we must turn to each other, and listen. We must reach toward others far away, and listen. Despite my country's aggressive response, I believe democracy and freedom now are about the power to listen.

America has been wounded twice in recent history: first the numerical faltering of November 2000, when our electoral system teetered in uncertainty. And then September 11, 2001, when our planes took the lives of our own. As the old woman at Amana told me, "The winds of change, they are blowing, and we feel them."

For the writer, the teacher, and the seeker, the events of our time have a common remedy—a remedy more difficult than war, but also more effective—and it resides in how we embrace the voices around us to find vision and establish a new democracy. Is it naive to seek constructive remedy with the likes of poetry and song from the voices of the people? I find it more foolish to seek lasting remedy with military power and a return to the status quo: "Keep America rolling." This approach may build consumer confidence, and breed new terror, but will not initiate new forms of economy and reconciliation. Without new vision, we will perish. Maybe now, at this distance, it is time to consider what the election of 2000 means today, and what that meaning offers us for the years beyond September 11, 2001.

On election night 2000, as I listened, flipping the channels, to the frenzied commentaries, I heard much I have forgotten. But as the great tidal tug of numbers, predictions, and alternating partisan euphoria and despair swept across the screen, one of the many voices on the many channels said something I will not forget, although I have forgotten the speaker's name: "The campaign between Al Gore and George W. Bush was devoid of poetry."

Poetry? When asked to explain, the commentator said that neither candidate called on us to sacrifice anything, to suffer for a greater good, or have the courage to do something difficult. Neither gave us a vision of how we might become more than we had been. The speaker's colleagues disagreed, but I thought the absence of poetry in this sense was the right explanation for a lack of substance in the whole campaign, and for the lack of resolution in the outcome.

The next morning, as it became clear there was no true winner, an odd idea came to me: The failure to elect a clear leader signals that each citizen becomes a leader. An election is a kind of abdication by each voter, after all, a handoff of responsibility from citizen to candidate. This system is insufficient, denying democracy rather than fulfilling it. Collectively, we all must lead.

The 2000 election, it turned out, was not about the consolidation of power, but about the distribution of opportunity for leadership.

New leadership, wherever it resides, will benefit from democratic expression broadly shared. For we have left the time of the stranger behind, the time when it was okay not to know how it is for people far away who suffer. Now each life becomes ambassador to all by hearing and speaking local visions, poems, stories, and songs. Our utterances will be judged not by their verbal mastery but by their importance — by the welcome they receive and the constructive social effects they enable. For the work of our time is the power to listen, to understand, to contribute — not to prove, or to prevail. I would call this "Article 0" of the U.S. Constitution: Stepping apart from received authority, we articulate new visions and collective responsibilities, and then we live them.

Let the great lumbering machine of politics and government go forward, I say, and let the president seek bipartisan support for the ongoing prerogatives of government. I wish him well. At the same time, however, let the leadership of the country shift toward the expressive power of individuals everywhere. Let the nation's leaders hear from their constituents not for-and-against opinions to be tallied, but generative ideas, lyric clarities, and memorable words of witness to be understood. "Bipartisan" is too narrow a way to describe what we need. I want some new glory of international inclusion to accompany the old glory of patriotism. I want kinship founded in the power to listen and share as well as to strategize and convince.

Let the age of information be succeeded by the age of insight, and of democratic expression. This will be the bright side of electoral failure. Our life becomes something that Mikhail Gorbachev has been suggesting for some time: Leadership today consists of being a good partner — in your family, your neighborhood, your country, and your world. Leadership is about listening for ideas that will lead us in common directions.

What might this new paradigm for democracy be? When entropy has worn down the old system, where lies the creative spark for the new? I believe the spark is widely distributed, and easily available, but long overlooked.

All my life I have been listening to people around me, and I have so relished the little texts I hear that I have come to think of my role in life as a collector of evocative "language from the world," as an anthologist of uncommon voices. People say important things, and in memorable words—ideas of value far beyond their origin. Local utterance can have national value. Certain local stories, in fact, are international. I want to honor citizens who combine local insight and a broad view.

Shortly after September 11, 2001, for example, a certain poem by the Palestinian American writer Naomi Shihab Nye began to appear posted in the streets in Jerusalem. Naomi had published her poem in English, but these copies appeared in English, Arabic, and Hebrew:

I'm not interested in
who suffered the most.
I'm interested in
people getting over it. . . .

There's a place in this brain
where hate won't grow.
I touch its riddle: wind, and seeds.
Something pokes us as we sleep.

It's late but everything comes next.

That, for me, typifies the work of our time—a collaboration between a spontaneous effort by neighbors in the world and the eloquence of one. We work together. Sometimes the text will have a folk origin, and the writer will be its messenger to a broader audience, and sometimes the process will happen the other way around—the professional writer becoming known in a new way in local places.

In my studio is a box I have labeled "language from the world," which holds treasures gleaned from twenty years of listening, watching, and taking dictation on voices I have overheard. Many of these texts are anonymous, and they have been published by being given away or posted in public places. This is the samizdat of the world, and I believe my box holds a representative sample of our future collective life: democratic texts created and shared outside the tangle of fame, greed, and cult of personality that can restrict the authenticity and effectiveness of formal artistry.

One example to begin: In Oregon, years ago, we lost seven students and two teachers in a mountain-climbing accident. Shortly after the tragedy, I received by mail a cassette tape from someone I didn't know, and without any explanatory message. There was just this one voice, singing:

There's nine lovely angels in heaven tonight,
Expelled in the darkness by God's holy light.
There's nothing more glorious, more breathing, nor bright
Than nine lovely angels in heaven tonight.

By a number penciled on the cassette label, I called the composer, and an old man's voice answered.

"You sent me the song of the nine lovely angels," I said. "How did you come to make that?"

"I was so deeply troubled," he said, "by what happened to those children, I stayed up all of a long night to make that song. And then I was moved to send it to you."

"Would you mind if I shared your song with others?" I said.

"If you are so moved."

Sometimes a letter from a friend reaches far beyond my own need, and I want to publish the compact clarity one voice has revealed. Recently, Native American writer Elizabeth Woody sent me a note concluding,

> Our people have a genius, or great intelligence, or we are part of a great intelligence that shows us what we must do. It doesn't matter to whom it speaks, bloodwise. If we love and honor one another, the experience grows and cycles back and with less effort than when we first consciously "tried" to acquire knowledge, things fall in place. The Earth has a voice and its own requirements that really are stronger than weakness, or loneliness, or even greed in all its forms. I am learning myself, all the time, and am grateful, even though I feel my limits nagging at me.

She had invited me to listen for ways to increase my belonging on this continent.

I can hear my friends challenge me: So what? These are dispensable fragments.

Well, I reply, shall we let the election of 2000 be the big bang of our national universe, the time we let our differences send us flying apart? Shall we let terror simplify the world to good and evil? Or shall we lean toward one another, recognize our need, and cherish all magnetic nudges toward inclusion?

The Bushmen of the Kalahari, I am told, being a small, inventive people, live by a proverb the world proves to them: "Things are powerful in proportion to their smallness." I find this true for the impact of language on public life. Short texts get through, get passed on, get remembered, and so are available for application at exactly the right moment. How do you recognize that moment? It is now. Now the duty of the seeker is to be what the tradition of Islam calls a *mesaharati,* a public waker. With an evocative message the *mesaharati* goes through the streets before dawn to wake all citizens, and call them to prayer. Not to tell them what to pray, but to call on them to pray. Perhaps I have appointed myself in this role. Or perhaps it was my father who appointed me.

My father, William Stafford, published fifty books of poetry, including one that received the National Book Award in 1963: *Traveling through the Dark*. Every morning he would rise before first light to write, lying on the couch alone, gazing into the dark, then scribbling:

> The grace we need to find will not be found by the graceful only.

> Successful people are in a rut.

> Once you decide to do right, life is easy—no distractions.

> The greatest ownership of all is to glance around and understand.

In the 1950s he wrote "Thinking for Berky," a poem about a girl who suffered terrible things:

> In the late night listening from bed
> I have joined the ambulance or the patrol
> screaming toward some drama, the kind of end
> that Berky must have some day, if she isn't dead. . . .

He thought for Berky, spoke for Berky. Her life was his source. And then toward the end of the poem, my father made an assessment of America:

> We live in an occupied country, misunderstood.
> Justice will take us millions of intricate moves. . . .

The 2000 presidential election, in all its confusion, taught me again what justice will take: millions of moves, each so intricate the greatest leaders in the land cannot accomplish them alone. And after terror, what do we do? Again, more than grand warlike gestures we need infinite moves, and these can only be accomplished by infinite hands.

That's good. Let's embrace our millions of moves to understand. Let's make each vote the size of a voice, and hear from each voice the poetry of compact, democratic insight.

What I call poetry here is the power to say something magnificent and eloquent in a small space. The small thing gives meaning to the great. A single evocative idea will always have more power to change lives than the entirety of the Congressional Record. Why? I believe for the same reason our eyes are designed to focus on a single human face, not a multitude. We best live as if face to face, though we may be distant and many.

On the computer screen, in this time, something very practical might begin to happen. The currency of peace may be our writings on that screen just the size of a song—little stories where we learn to pronounce our feelings, blessings the size of a lullaby, a letter, an inclusive manifesto, a notably eloquent posting on the Web. For in our time there is a great thing not yet done. It is the marriage of Woody Guthrie's gusto and the Internet.

According to his son Arlo, the most productive period in Woody Guthrie's life was the month he spent in Oregon writing songs on the payroll of the Bonneville Power Administration. He wrote twenty-seven songs in thirty days. His example makes me ambitious. The e-mail box on my screen, after all, is the size of a folk song, a lullaby, a love poem. What treasure could I put there, not to sell or capture or overcome anything, but simply to offer? What treasure could any of us put there, something we have held secret until now?

A friend told me we spend the majority of our energy *not* doing what we most *want* to do, not saying what we want to say. Most energy, she said, serves to keep the lid on. The soul waits, the heart waits. But when we write, even a note, we let out soul. There may be no other way than the short truth, a shock of clear words.

When Dick Cheney was Secretary of Defense, he came to Portland, Oregon, to give a keynote address for an organization called the World Affairs Council. Through some fluke in the selection process the council had decided to give an award to two citizens from Portland: Phil Knight, CEO of Nike (for his contributions to world understanding through international business), and me (for my contributions to world understanding through teaching). The fact that my contributions had been quite modest somehow bypassed the selection committee, and there I was at the awards-banquet head table with Phil, Dick, and several others. I realized as the plates were swept away that I was about to give a speech to Dick Cheney. Following his keynote, the mistress of ceremonies would invite Phil to the podium to accept his award, and then me. My acceptance speech would be my chance.

Secretary Cheney chose as his keynote theme "The Assets of Security," which turned out to include an array of innovative weaponry: catastrophic submarines, smart weapons operated from remote points, and other terrors. As I listened, another list began to form in my mind, what might be called "the assets of peace"—beginning with childhood, music, food, personal letters, compassion, parenting at home and across boundaries, the urge to dance, and poetry. As this list passed through my mind, a frightening mathematical formula presented itself. Dick Cheney had been my muse.

Phil Knight, as I remember, accepted his award with a brief comment. He has many chances to address the multitude. But this was my one. When I rose to accept the award, my words came forth like this:

We live in a world where a few people could destroy us all. But a few people could not save us. The math doesn't work that way. The only way we can be saved is for many people, and finally all people, to recognize and live by interdependence on earth. Even though they are not funded as such, education, language study, the arts, and cultural exchanges among the divided populations of the world are the highest priority of our time. These are the assets of peace.

I couldn't tell that my little speech made much of an impression on the secretary. But to measure its importance by his reaction alone would be foreign to what I was understanding there. It was not the leaders who needed to understand this from me, it was the leaders of the leaders—the people.

Inviting into our lives the habit of speaking, writing, and sharing what we hear around us can have all kinds of unanticipated consequences, and one is a feeling that one might make a difference in the world. Do I harbor delusions of grandeur? I don't want fame. I want to participate in the work of our time by joining others to smuggle ideas into the culture at large.

It's no accident that the most widely admired texts of our political history are short. Fragments, really. They are the poems of our political discourse:

Four score and seven years ago.

The hand that rocks the cradle can rock the boat.

The only thing we have to fear is fear itself.

Ask not what your country can do for you.

In the past I thought I was a writer, and a writing teacher. But now I find I am a listener who uses the act of writing to identify and pass along gifts that come to me. As a teacher I want my students to be active in the spirit of the elder I heard at the Root Feast on the Warm Springs Indian Reservation:

Down on the corner was a song, waiting to see if anyone would hear it. In my heart was a song, waiting to see if I would hear it. I have heard it! I would sing it now for you.

A song, waiting—what is it for you? Where is our song for Martin Luther King? What do we sing to our children of Mother Teresa? What song do we use to teach our children the ways of Bobby Kennedy? What song could bring home to our children the lives of children in Afghanistan, Iraq, Israel, and Palestine?

The real meaning of democratic citizenship is the search for some form of song that enables the individual life to enter the world. When the anthropologist Ruth Underhill asked her Papago informant, María Chona, about the meaning of a particular Papago song, María replied: "Our songs are short because we understand so much." Then she proceeded to elaborate her tiny song into a cosmic story.

The short songs we need now are about to be written by voices we don't yet know. We will need to be eloquent listeners to invite these songs forth, and share them all around.

When I was a child, my parents would remind us, "Don't forget to talk to strangers." How else could we be helped if we got lost, or hurt? And how else could we be citizens of the world? Our millions of intricate moves may be as direct and simple as making songs and learning from strangers.

THERE WAS A TIME

There was a time when art was but a decoration,
    when music in the background was the rule.
There were times when culture was a way to sweeten days
    like fine cuisine.
We knew times when poetry murmured
    in a classroom, once the real work had been done,
    when a book at home was something we might use
    to put ourselves to sleep.

A storm of terror cleared all that—again.
And now we live by killing far away.

Art is not a weapon but a hand.
Is it naive to reach for justice with a poem, a story,
    or a song?
Not so foolish, I say, as promise lasting safety, prosperity,
    or any shred of true abundance in a child's long life
    by striking back.

Art must be like breath, catching at the brim of fear
    to inspire the next epoch of our life together.
Can money do that? An army? The greatest power in the world?

Be honest: Rivers find each other by seeking the meeting place.
Live there. Take up the pen.

Acknowledgments

One morning when I woke in the forest, I looked up to first light at the tops of the trees and I could feel their gratitude. I could feel their green surge of thanks for the sunlight, for the earth, for water. And I could feel their affinity for one another. It was a very quiet feeling, ordinary, a sensation of every morning. I will never forget.

In making this book, I have that feeling again. How many people have helped me, how many places have shaped me? As this book tries to tell, the muses are all around us, and over the years this book has become a home for stories and ideas from many sources. My students are so hungry to speak their spirits, they gift me with treasure. I can't name them all, but their stories are who I am. And with these students, it has been my privilege to teach since 1986 at the Northwest Writing Institute, a part of the Graduate School of Education at Lewis and Clark College in Oregon. In the institute, my teaching companions spill ideas and insights like thistledown exploding in the wind. It's hard to tell after a while where ideas began, who first tried a certain kind of writing or teaching before we all tried variations. I would honor everyone there, not in this note but with this book.

Diane McDevitt has helped me see creative ministry in my administrative job. The institute, and this book, would not exist without her. And I am grateful to Lewis and Clark College for suffering us to pursue a mission that some might not understand, and for a sabbatical in 2000–2001 to complete this book.

I am grateful to the Fishtrap Writers Gathering and the Sitka Center for Art and Ecology for the chance to teach exploratory workshops, and for refuge to complete the writing. I am also grateful to the editors of the following magazines for previously publishing chapters from this book: *Teachers and Writers Magazine, Mossy Creek Journal, News from the Loft,* the *Voice* and the *Quarterly* of the National Writing Project, the newsletter of the Wyoming Arts Commission, and *American Art.* "The Writer as Professional Eavesdropper" was published in a different form in *Writer's Craft, Teacher's Art,* edited by Mimi Schwartz (Portsmouth, N.H.: Boynton/Cook, 1991). "The Good Son" was published in *Writing Path 2: Poetry and Prose from Writers' Conferences,* edited by Michael Pettit (Iowa City: University of Iowa Press, 1996), and in *Harper's.* "Rosie's Book of Sayings" appeared in an earlier form in *The Alphabet of the Trees: A Guide to Nature Writing,* edited by Christian McEwen and Mark Statman (New York: Teachers and Writers Collaborative, 2000).

Jim Hepworth, Margot Thompson, and Richard Sterling helped in particular ways, and my three agents over the span of this book's making—Elizabeth Grossman, Jennie McDonald, and Doug Stewart —have been winsome listeners to my stories and ideas for a decade, encouraging me to "Write that down, and send it to me." Paul Merchant was especially helpful as I searched for the shape of this book.

I am grateful to my editor Barbara Ras for seeing this book more as a letter to the life of our time than simply a text about the act of writing, and to Courtney Denney for her copyediting.

Finally, this book is for my wife. In the writing life, there is much not knowing. Like the tide, I advance and ebb. Perrin believes.